The
INTERCESSORY
PRAYER
of
JESUS

Other Titles by Warren W. Wiersbe (selected)

Being a Child of God
Be Myself
The Bible Exposition Commentary (2 vols.)
The Bumps Are What You Climb On
Developing a Christian Imagination
Elements of Preaching
God Isn't in a Hurry: Learning to Slow Down and Live
Living with the Giants: The Lives of Great Men of the Faith
Meet Yourself in the Psalms
On Being a Servant of God
Prayer, Praise, and Promises: A Daily Walk through the
    Psalms
Run with the Winners
So That's What a Christian Is! 12 Pictures of the Dynamic
    Christian Life
The Strategy of Satan
Turning Mountains into Molehills: And Other Devotional
    Talks
Victorious Christians You Should Know
Wiersbe's Expository Outlines on the New Testament
Wiersbe's Expository Outlines on the Old Testament
Windows on the Parables

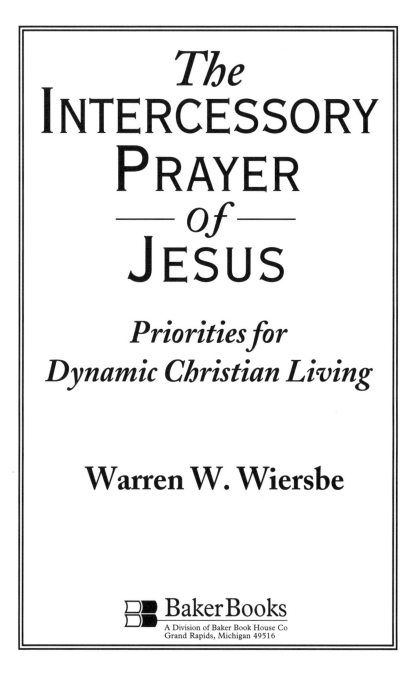

The INTERCESSORY PRAYER — *of* — JESUS

Priorities for Dynamic Christian Living

Warren W. Wiersbe

Baker Books

A Division of Baker Book House Co
Grand Rapids, Michigan 49516

Published by Baker Books
a division of Baker Book House Company
P.O. Box 6287, Grand Rapids, MI 49516-6287

Printed in the United States of America

Library of Congress Cataloging-in-Publication Data

Wiersbe, Warren W.
    The intercessory prayer of Jesus : priorities for dynamic Christian
living / Warren W. Wiersbe.
      p.   cm.
    ISBN 0-8010-5779-5
    1. Bible N.T. John XVII—Commentaries. I. Title.
BS2615.3.W53   1997
226.5'06—dc21   97-13784

For information about academic books, resources for Christian leaders, and
all new releases available from Baker Book House, visit our web site:
http://www.bakerbooks.com

Dedicated to the memory of my friend
Philip R. Newell

For many years Director of the
Great Commission Prayer League

A man of prayer who encouraged
many of us to ask God for the things
that matter most.

CONTENTS

PREFACE

he time has come for the church to get its priorities in order, and one of the best ways to do this is to find out what was important to Jesus Christ. John 17—our Lord's "High Priestly Prayer"—tells us what his priorities were and are.

This book is not a *detailed* exposition of John 17. It is a practical study of the major themes of this profound prayer. Much of this material was given in a radio series over "Back to the Bible Broadcast" during February and March 1982. However, I have recast the entire series since it is possible to write things in a book that may not be spoken over the air.

My prayer is that God will use these studies to get the church back on course. There is a price to pay, but there will be a greater price if we continue to drift.

Each of us must do his part, no matter the cost.

Warren W. Wiersbe

1

THE GREATEST PRAYER EVER PRAYED

Some brethren pray by the yard; but true prayer is measured by weight, and not by length."

So spoke the British Baptist preacher Charles Haddon Spurgeon; *and he is right!* The greatest prayer ever prayed is recorded in John 17, and it takes about six minutes to reverently read it aloud. There is not much length, but there is certainly a great deal of depth and weight! According to Dr. Herbert Lockyer Sr., there are 650 definite prayers recorded in the Bible; but not one of them can match our Lord's "High Priestly Prayer" in John 17—nor can any prayer recorded *outside* the Bible.

What is it about this prayer that makes it so great? Let me suggest four reasons.

1. *It is great because of the person who prayed the prayer.*

This person is none other than Jesus Christ, the Son of God. Not only is he the Son of God, but he is God the Son, eternal God come to earth in human, but sinless, flesh.

11

Each of the four Gospels has its own special emphasis. Matthew emphasizes Christ the King, the Messiah promised in the Old Testament Scriptures. Mark is the Gospel of the Servant, and Luke pictures the sympathetic Son of man. But John's purpose in writing is to present the deity of Jesus Christ. "Many other signs therefore Jesus also performed in the presence of the disciples, which are not written in this book; but these have been written that you may believe that Jesus is the Christ, the Son of God; and that believing you may have life in His name" (John 20:30–31).

This explains why John included this prayer in his Gospel: it magnifies the awesome truth that Jesus Christ is eternal God. Almost every verse in John 17 expresses this great fact.

Only God the Son could ask the Father to glorify him (v. 1). Moses asked to *see* God's glory (Exod. 33:18). Jesus asked to *receive* God's glory, and he identified it as the same glory which he had with the Father "before the world was" (v. 5). Only an unbalanced person, or eternal God, would claim to have glory or anything else "before the world was."

Furthermore, only God can give sinners eternal life (v. 2). And note in verse 3 that Jesus put himself on an equal basis with God. The sinner receives eternal life when he comes to know by faith "the only true God, and Jesus Christ. . . ." Put anybody else's name in there and see if it makes sense. In this simple statement, Jesus claimed to be God.

Four times in this prayer, Jesus said that God the Father sent him (vv. 3, 18, 21, 25). Of course, any apostle or prophet can claim to be sent by God; but no mere human being could claim that he *came forth from God* (v. 8, and see John 16:28). Any Christian could pray, "All things that are Mine are Thine"; but only the Son of God could add "and Thine are Mine" (v. 10). Jesus claimed to possess everything that the Father possessed! He also claimed to be *one with the Father* (vv. 11 and 21).

12

The very manner in which Jesus prayed reveals that he is God. He did not begin "Our Father" but simply, "Father." *Jesus never prayed, "Our Father."* Jesus told Mary Magdalene on that first Easter morning, "Go to My brethren, and say to them, 'I ascend to My Father and your Father, and My God and your God'" (John 20:17). God is *our* Father by grace, but He is Jesus' Father by nature. And the word that Jesus used for "pray" (vv. 9, 15, 20) is not the common word for "pray" in the New Testament. The word means "to request *from an equal.*" You and I could not use this word because we are not equal with God. But Jesus used it three times! Why? Because he is eternal God.

In verse 24, Jesus boldly said, "Father, I will. . . ." (KJV). It was not a request; it was a command. Believers today cannot pray with that kind of authority. Such praying would not be faith; it would be presumption. But God the Son can address God the Father in that manner because they are equals. *Jesus is God!*

There are other evidences of our Lord's deity in this prayer, but we will stop with verse 24: "for Thou didst love Me before the foundation of the world." While it is true that God loves his people "with an everlasting love" (Jer. 31:3), he cannot express that love to them until they are actually existing on the earth. But the Father loved the Son from all eternity. Eternal glory and eternal love are brought together in verse 24.

If anyone else prayed in this manner and made these claims, we would conclude that he was either confused or mentally disturbed. Only Jesus Christ, God the Son, could pray this way.

But this great truth that Jesus Christ is God introduces a bit of a problem: Why would *God* pray? The Gospel records present Jesus Christ as a man of prayer. I have counted at least nineteen instances in the Gospels of Jesus praying. Is there not a contradiction here? No, because when

Jesus was ministering on earth, he did *everything* in total dependence on the Father. Jesus said, "As the living Father sent Me, and I live because of the Father. . . ." (John 6:57). His works and his words came from the Father (John 5:36 and 14:24). Day by day, Jesus depended on the Father. Satan tempted Jesus to use his divine power for himself; but Jesus refused to yield (Matt. 4:1–11).

In other words, our Lord lived by faith and depended on prayer during his life and ministry on earth. Now if Jesus Christ, with all of his power and perfection, had to depend on prayer, how much more do you and I, with our multiplied imperfections and weaknesses, need to depend on prayer!

The French essayist Montaigne wrote: "There are few men who durst publish to the world the prayers they make to Almighty God." Jesus Christ has given us this prayer, and we thank God that he did!

2. *It is great because of the occasion that demanded the prayer.*
"That's one small step for a man, one giant leap for mankind." If Neil Armstrong had made that statement while playing hopscotch with the neighborhood children, nobody would have paid any attention to him. But he made that statement as he stepped from his spacecraft, as the first man to walk on the moon. The situation helped to give weight to his words.

What was our Lord's situation and how did it relate to this prayer?

To begin with, Jesus had just finished instructing his disciples (John 13–16). Now he prayed for them, because prayer and the Word of God go together. If we have all Bible but no prayer, we may have a great deal of truth but no power. It would be "light without heat." On the other hand, if we have all prayer but no Bible teaching, we are in danger of becoming fanatics—heat without light! Zeal is a good thing, but zeal without knowledge is usually destructive.

A proper balance of Bible study and prayer is important to a balanced Christian life. "Moreover, as for me," said the godly prophet Samuel, "far be it from me that I should sin against the LORD by ceasing to pray for you; but I will instruct you in the good and right way" (1 Sam. 12:23). Note the balance of prayer and the Word of God. "And now I commend you to God [that's prayer] and to the word of His grace, which is able to build you up. . . ." (Acts 20:32). Paul knew the importance of spiritual balance, and so did the other apostles: "But we will devote ourselves to prayer, and to the ministry of the word" (Acts 6:4).

The only way the Word of God can become real in our lives is through prayer and obedience. One reason we have unbalanced Christians in our churches is the lack of prayer to back up the study of God's Word. It is much easier to get Christians to attend a Bible study than a prayer meeting, and yet we need both. Jesus *taught* his disciples, and then he *prayed* for them.

But this prayer was not only for the disciples; it was also for Jesus Christ. Remember, he was facing the cross. When our Lord began his ministry and was baptized, he prayed to the Father (Luke 3:21). Throughout his ministry, he prayed to the Father (Luke 3:21). Throughout his ministry, he depended on prayer. He arose early in the morning to pray (Mark 1:35) and even prayed all night (Luke 6:12). He prayed on the Mount of Transfiguration (Luke 9:28). Now he was praying as he faced the agony of Calvary.

The fact that Jesus prayed for himself in the first five verses of John 17 does not mean that he prayed a selfish prayer. This is the difference. If Jesus had not prayed for the Father to glorify him and receive him back into heaven, you and I would have no salvation today. In praying for himself, he was praying for us.

15

Think of what it must have meant to the Savior to commune with his Father! The cup he was about to drink would come from the Father's hand (John 18:11). There would be shame, pain, even death and temporary separation from the Father; but Jesus was not afraid. For this purpose he had come into the world, and the Father would see him through to glorious victory.

It is interesting to contrast this occasion of prayer with some of the other occasions of intercession recorded in the Scriptures. In Genesis 18 we read that Abraham interceded for the city of Sodom. But Jesus was burdened for *a whole world* and would die to save lost sinners. Moses interceded for a whole nation, the people of Israel (Exod. 32), and even offered to die that they might be forgiven. But Jesus did die! And because of his death, all who will trust him are forgiven and saved eternally. Solomon prayed a long prayer (1,050 words in our King James Version) in his dedication of the temple; but our Lord's prayer in John 17 meant the creation of a *spiritual* temple, the church (1 Peter 2:5).

Our Lord gives us a good example here: prayer is essential, not only in the everyday affairs of life, but especially in the crises of life. "Do not pray for easy lives," said Phillips Brooks. "Pray to be stronger men. Do not pray for tasks equal to your powers. Pray for powers equal to your tasks."

3. *It is great because of the petitions in the prayer.*

Prayer that asks nothing accomplishes nothing. We sing in one of our familiar hymns:

> *Thou art coming to a King,*
> *Large petitions with thee bring.*
> *For His grace and power are such,*
> *None can ever ask too much.*
> —John Newton

If ever there was a "kingly prayer," it is this one recorded in John 17. While the outline of the prayer is simple, the petitions in the prayer are profound. The prayer may be outlined as follows:

I. Jesus prayed for himself (1–5)
II. Jesus prayed for his disciples (6–19)
   A. Their security (6–12)
   B. Their sanctity (13–19)
III. Jesus prayed for the whole church (20–26)

The petitions in this prayer take us back to eternity past (v. 5) and forward into future glory in heaven (v. 24). This prayer deals with the glory of the Father and the Son (v. 1) as well as the church glorifying God on earth (v. 10). Our Lord mentions the Father's love for him (v. 24) as well as the Father's love for believers (v. 23).

Four words summarize the main requests in this prayer: glory, security, sanctity, and unity.

In verses 1–5, Jesus requested that the Father give to him the glory that he veiled when he (Jesus) came to earth. If God had not answered this request, none of the other requests could have been answered.

In the next section of the prayer (vv. 6–19), our Lord prayed for the disciples. He had two major concerns: their *security* (vv. 6–12: "Keep them") and their *sanctity* (vv. 13–19: "Sanctify them"). The disciples were the "pioneers" in world evangelism (v. 18) and needed all the prayer support they could get!

The final section emphasizes the whole church (vv. 20–26), and the major request is that God's people might experience *unity*: "That they all may be one. . . ." (v. 21).

These four requests—God's glory, and the security, sanctity, and unity of God's church—are good guidelines to follow in our own prayer life. Too much of our praying is shallow and selfish. Keeping these requests in mind could help us to deepen our own praying.

As you study this prayer, you will discover that Jesus Christ has given us three wonderful gifts. He has given us eternal life (v. 2), God's Word (vv. 8 and 14), and God's glory (v. 22). Because we have eternal life, we have *salvation*. The Word of God makes possible our *sanctification* (note v. 17), and our *glorification* is sure because he has already given us the glory. The believer's past, present, and future are secure!

An evangelist friend of mine told me about a teenager who wrecked the family car and stood by the wreckage praying, "O Lord, may this accident not have happened!" What a foolish prayer! Yet you and I have perhaps prayed some silly, shallow prayers. It is only as we grow in our knowledge of the Word of God that we can deepen our prayer life. It is when we test our requests by the Word of God that we discover how to pray in the will of God.

4. *It is great because of the victory it can give us today.*

A friend of mine wrote a thesis on the prayer of Solomon when he dedicated the temple. It is a marvelous prayer, but not a great deal in that prayer is applicable to New Testament believers today. Jesus prayed this prayer in John 17 so that his disciples could hear him (v. 13). What he prayed about relates to us today.

Jesus closed his upper room teaching with these words: "In the world you have tribulation, but take courage; I have overcome the world" (John 16:33). In his prayer, Jesus used the word "world" nineteen times! The prayer recorded in John 17 tells us how we can overcome the world. Let's put these two key verses together so we can get the full impact of what our Lord said.

In the world you have tribulation, but take courage, I have overcome the world.	. . . these things I speak in the world, that they may have My joy made full in themselves.

What we learn from his prayer gives us the courage to overcome the world, and the joy of this victory fills and controls our lives!

The word "world" is used in several different senses in Scripture. Sometimes it means "the created universe," as in John 17:5: "before the world was." Sometimes the word simply means "people, humanity," as in John 3:16: "For God so loved the world. . . ." But often the word "world" goes beyond creation and humanity and means "society organized without God and against God." When Jesus prayed, "they [the disciples] are not of the world, even as I am not of the world" (v. 14), he was using "world" in this sense. Theologians call this the "ethical use" of the word "world."

"The world" is the system of things that you and I used to belong to before we were saved. We lived "according to the course of this world" (Eph. 2:2). Our standards were the standards of this world, and our pleasures and satisfaction came from this world. When we trusted Jesus Christ as Savior, we received citizenship in heaven (Phil. 3:20–21) so that we no longer belong to this world system. We are in this world physically, but we do not belong to this world spiritually. Like a diver on the ocean floor we are out of our element, but we are able to survive because we have outside help.

What are the characteristics of this world system from which we have been delivered, yet against which we must constantly battle?

For one thing, we live in a *deceived* world. The world does not know God. In spite of all the world's wisdom, it cannot find God. (Read John 17:25 and 1 Cor. 1:18–31.) As far as the world is concerned, "one religion is just as good as another." The world is willing to accept the cross as a "religious symbol," but it has no concept of the person of the cross, or the purpose and power of the cross. "For the word of the cross is to those who are perishing foolishness. . . ." (1 Cor. 1:18).

The world is deceived because Satan, the prince of this world, deceives the mind and darkens the heart (2 Cor. 4:3–6; also see John 12:31; 14:30; and 16:11). "We know that we are of God, and the whole world lies in the power of the evil one" (1 John 5:19). Satan is a counterfeiter who provides religious substitutes for those who do not know Jesus Christ. "It makes no difference what you believe," says the world, "just so long as you believe something!"

In contrast to the deception that controls people in the world system, the believer has received the gift of eternal life, and he therefore shares in *reality*. "And this is eternal life," prayed Jesus, "that they may know Thee, the only true God, and Jesus Christ whom Thou has sent" (v. 3). *The only true God!* We overcome the world and share in Christ's joy because we have experienced reality: *we know the only true God!* And because we know the only true God, and his Son Jesus Christ, we do not need the substitutes that so excite the world. Our joy is found only in that which comes from the heart of the Father.

The world system is not only deceived, but it is also *dangerous*. "And the world is passing away. . . ." (1 John 2:17); "the form of this world is passing away" (1 Cor. 7:31). The people who are caught in the world system think it is safe, solid, enduring, and dependable, when in reality the world is temporary and passing. People say, "It's as sure as the world!" But nothing could be more *unsure* than this world system. (For that matter, the *created* world is not that sure. "Heaven and earth will pass away, but My words shall not pass away" [Matt. 24:35].)

Because the world is deceptive, it is dangerous. The world can even deceive God's own people and lead them into trouble. "Do not love the world, nor the things in the world" warned the apostle John (1 John 2:15). "And do not be conformed to this world," wrote the apostle Paul (Rom. 12:2). James asked the pertinent question, "Do you not know that friendship with the world is hostility toward God?" (James 4:4). "Make every effort to come to me soon," Paul wrote to Timothy, "for Demas, having loved this present world, has deserted me. . . ." (2 Tim. 4:9–10).

Satan is the prince of the world. He has declared war on God's people. "Be of sober spirit, be on the alert," Peter wrote. "Your adversary, the devil, prowls about like a roaring lion, seeking someone to devour" (1 Peter 5:8). Lions are dangerous! Satan will use the world to entice the believer out of the will of God.*

We not only live in a deceived and dangerous world, but we live in a *defiled* world. The believer must be careful to keep himself "unstained by the world" (James 1:27). The new nature that we have within creates new desires and new appetites, but there are always around us the temptations to lower things. Because of this new nature, believers have "escaped the corruption that is in the world by lust" (2 Peter 1:4), but they can still be tempted and they can still fall.

It is getting more and more difficult for us to keep ourselves "unstained by the world." We are invaded by the messengers of "the lust of the flesh and the lust of the eyes and the boastful pride of life" (1 John 2:16). Whether the advertisers are promoting automobiles or artichokes, they seem to need the help of sex and pride to get their message across. Seductively dressed models who know nothing about the product try to woo us into making a purchase. Or perhaps it is the handsome businessman (obviously wealthy) who tries to inflate our ego and win us over. Stephen Leacock once described advertising as "the science of arresting the human intelligence long enough to get money from it."

---

*For a study of Satan and his tactics, see my book *The Strategy of Satan*, published by Tyndale House.

Finally, this present world is a *divided* world. Satan's purpose is to divide and conquer, and he seems to be succeeding. Even the saints have a hard time getting along with each other! We put labels on each other ("liberal," "fundamentalist," "neo-evangelical," "militant fundamentalist," "neo-fundamentalist," and so on) and think that our labels solve problems. Usually they create more problems, because most maturing Christians don't remain in the same pigeonhole very long, and some are difficult to categorize. We spend more time with the labels than we do with the people we are identifying!

Here, then, are four characteristics of the world we live in: it is a deceived world, a dangerous world, a defiled world, and a divided world. One of the messages of John 17 is how to overcome the world. Let's see what this prayer has to say to us about the world that we live in.

We live in a deceived world, but in Jesus Christ we have *reality*. We know and trust the "only true God." The gift of eternal life has put us in touch with reality. Our Lord mentioned this truth in verses 1–5. The better we know God the Father and his Son Jesus Christ the less interest we will have in the transient toys of the world system. "If any one loves the world, the love of the Father is not in him" (1 John 2:15). It is our love for the Father that fills our life with spiritual reality.

We live in a dangerous world, but we are secure in Jesus Christ (vv. 6–12). Because he has manifested God's name to us (and this means God's nature, God's character), we are not afraid. "The name of the LORD is a strong tower; the righteous runs into it and is safe" (Prov. 18:10). Jesus prayed, "Holy Father, keep them in Thy name. . . ." (v. 11).

We live in a defiled world, but it is possible to keep pure because of our relationship to Jesus Christ. In verses 13–19, our Lord prayed for our sanctification. He gave us the gift of his Word to enable us to walk in the way of holiness. "Sanctify them in the truth; Thy word is truth" (v. 17).

We live in a divided world, but in Jesus Christ we who are saved have spiritual unity (vv. 20–26). To enable us to preserve and promote this unity, he gave us the gift of his glory (v. 22). We do not need to manufacture spiritual unity: the unity is already there and all we must do is maintain it.

Perhaps a summary chart would make these truths more clear.

The world we live in	God's provision in Jesus Christ
A deceived world	The gift of eternal life (1–5): We have reality.
A dangerous world	The revelation of God's name (6–12): We have security.
A defiled world	The gift of the Word (13–19): We have sanctity.
A divided world	The gift of God's glory (20–26): We have unity.

The famous American preacher, Henry Ward Beecher, once said, "It is not well for a man to pray cream and live skim milk." The important thing about our study of John 17 is that it makes a difference in our daily lives. One of the tests of whether or not we are personally benefiting from this study is, "What is my attitude toward the world?" As we study, we must take inventory of our lives. Are we being deceived by something in the world and thus being robbed of the reality in Christ? Are we putting ourselves into a place of danger that could ruin our testimony, our work, our home? Are we secretly being defiled by the world? Are we creating unbiblical divisions instead of encouraging spiritual unity?

23

After all, we are not blessed for our studying of the Word, but for our *doing* of the Word.

"But one who looks intently at the perfect law, the law of liberty, and abides by it . . . this man shall be blessed in what he does" (James 1:25).

Prayer: Basic Training

These things Jesus spoke; and lifting up His eyes to heaven, He said, "Father, the hour has come; glorify Thy Son, that the Son may glorify Thee."

—John 17:1

Lord, teach us to pray!"

This request from one of the disciples (Luke 11:1) gave evidence of real spiritual insight. *We* must learn how to pray. While praying is as natural to the Christian as breathing is to a mammal, even breathing must be studied and practiced if it is to be correct. Public speakers work on their breathing so that they get the most out of their voice and don't injure it. The fact that we have been praying since childhood is no guarantee that we really know how to pray effectively.

John 17:1 gives us some guidelines to follow for effective praying.

1. *Posture is not important.*

Was our Lord kneeling or standing when he offered this prayer? We don't know. All we do know is that he lifted up his eyes to heaven (see John 11:41). Most people bow their heads and close their eyes when they pray, but Jesus lifted his head and focused his eyes on heaven. Many people fold their hands when they pray, but I don't find this practice anywhere in Scripture. In fact, the Jews were accustomed to lifting up their hands, open to God, expecting to receive something! (Note 1 Kings 8:22; Neh. 8:6; Ps. 28:2; and 1 Tim. 2:8.)

Many different prayer postures are recorded in the Bible, and all of them are acceptable. Some people bowed their knees when they prayed (Gen. 24:52; 2 Chron. 20:18; Eph. 3:14). When Jesus prayed in Gethsemane, he began by bowing his knees (Luke 22:41). He then fell on his face as he talked to the Father (Matt. 26:39). It was Daniel's practice to kneel when he prayed (Dan. 6:10), but King David sat when he talked to God about the promised kingdom (2 Sam. 7:18). Abraham stood when he interceded for Sodom (Gen. 18:22). So there are many postures for prayer.

The important thing is *the posture of the heart.* It is much easier to bow the knees than to bow the heart in submission to God. While the outward posture can be evidence of the inward spiritual attitude, it is not always so. Again, the important thing is the posture of the heart.

2. *We pray to the Father.*

The biblical pattern for prayer is to the Father, in the name of the Son, in the power of the Spirit. Jesus addressed his Father six times in this prayer. (Some people say "Father" or "Lord" with every sentence that they pray. This is a bad habit that should be cured.) Four times he simply said "Father"; the other two times, he called him "Holy Father" and "righteous Father" (vv. 11 and 25). From this, I gather that it is not wrong for us to use suitable adjectives when we address our Father in heaven. However, we must be careful to mean what we say and not overdo it.

We address the Father, of course, because prayer is based on sonship. In what we traditionally call "The Lord's Prayer" (Matt. 6:9–13), Jesus taught his disciples to pray, "Our Father." Jesus never prayed "Our Father." We noted in chapter 1 that Jesus had a different relationship to the Father because he is the eternal Son of God. He said, "I ascend to My Father and your Father, and My God and your God" (John 20:17).

We hear people addressing their prayers to the Son and even to the Holy Spirit. Is this wrong? When Stephen gave his life for Christ, he saw Jesus in heaven and addressed his prayer to him: "Lord Jesus, receive my spirit!" (Acts 7:59). I know of no prayer in the Bible addressed to the Holy Spirit. Since our prayers are addressed to God, and since Father and Son and Holy Spirit are all in the Godhead, *technically* we can address our prayers to each of them. However, the biblical pattern seems to be that we pray to the Father, in the name of the Son, and through the power of the Spirit.

Nowhere in this prayer does our Lord mention the Holy Spirit. He had in his upper room discourse taught the disciples about the Holy Spirit (John 14:16–17, 26; 15:26; 16:7–13). Jude 20 instructs us to pray "in the Holy Spirit," which seems to relate to Romans 8:26–27, verses that every serious prayer warrior should ponder. We cannot expect God to answer unless we pray in his will (1 John 5:14–15). We discover the will of God primarily through the Word of God (Col. 1:9–10), and it is one of the ministries of the Spirit to teach us from the Word (John 16:13–14).

The fact that prayer is based on sonship suggests that the Father is obligated to listen when his children call. In fact, it is more than an obligation: it is the Father's *delight* when his children fellowship with him and share their needs. "If you then, being evil, know how to give good gifts to your children, how much more shall your Father who is in heaven give what is good to those who ask Him!" (Matt. 7:11). The Father's heart reaches out in love to his own, and he longs to share good things with them. And the better we know our Father, the easier it is to pray in his will.

3. *We must be yielded to the Father's will.*

A storm passed over the Florida coast and left a great deal of wreckage behind. The next day as the men were cleaning up their little town, one man said, "I'm not ashamed to admit that I prayed during that storm last night." One of his friends replied, "Yes, I'm sure the Lord heard many new voices last night."

Prayer is not like those little red boxes we see in buildings and occasionally on street corners, marked "USE ONLY IN EMERGENCY." I enjoy sharing good things with my children, but if they only spoke to me when they were in trouble or in need of something, our relationship would quickly deteriorate. Unless we do the will of God, our living will negate our praying.

"Father, the hour has come. . . ." What hour? The hour for which he had come into the world. The hour when he would die on the cross, be buried, rise again, and finish the great work of redemption. You may trace this "hour" in John's Gospel.

John 2:4	Woman, what do I have to do with you? My hour has not yet come.
John 7:30	They were seeking therefore to seize Him; and no man laid his hand on Him, because His hour had not yet come.
John 8:20	These words He spoke in the treasury, as He taught in the temple; and no one seized Him, because His hour had not yet come.

John 12:23	And Jesus answered them, saying, "The hour has come for the Son of Man to be glorified."
John 13:1	Now before the Feast of the Passover, Jesus knowing that His hour had come that He should depart out of this world to the Father, having loved His own to the end.
John 17:1	"Father, the hour has come. . . ."

I think it was Robert Law who said, "The purpose of prayer is not to get man's will done in heaven, but to get God's will done on earth." If we want to *pray* in the will of God, then we must *live* in the will of God. Prayer is not something that we *do*; it is something that we *are*. It is the highest and deepest expression of the inner person.

It is this profound relationship between practice and prayer that helps us understand such promises as Psalm 37:4: "Delight yourself in the LORD; And He will give you the desires of your heart." A superficial reading of this promise would lead you to believe that God is a doting Father who plays favorites with those who pamper him. But that is not what this promise says. If we delight in the Lord, and seek to please him in everything, then something is going to happen to our own desires. *His desires become our desires.* We start to say with our Lord, "My food is to do the will of Him who sent Me, and to accomplish His work" (John 4:34). Our praying, then, is simply the reflection of God's desires in our own heart.

There is a price to pay when we sincerely pray in the will of God. Jesus was about to receive the cup from his Father's hand (John 18:10–11). The Father had prepared the cup, and the hour had come. But Jesus was not afraid. Peter tried to protect the Master, but Jesus rebuked him. "The cup which the Father has given Me, shall I not drink it?" (John

18:11). We need never fear the will of God; and, if we are in the will of God, we need never fear the answers he gives to our prayers. If a son asks for bread, will he receive a stone? If he asks for a fish, will his father give him a snake?

Living in the will of God makes it possible for us to "pray without ceasing" (1 Thess. 5:17). This command obviously doesn't mean that we are to go around mumbling prayers. Our real praying is expressed by the desires of our heart. If our lips frame requests that are different from the desires in our heart, then we are praying hypocritically. God does not hear words; he sees hearts. So, when we live in the will of God, the desires of our heart should become more and more godly. These desires are really *prayers* that constantly ascend to the Lord.

Jesus lived on a divine timetable. When he told his disciples he was going back to Judea to help Mary, Martha, and Lazarus, the disciples protested. "Rabbi, the Jews were just now seeking to stone You, and are You going there again?" What was our Lord's reply? "Are there not twelve hours in the day?" (John 11:8–9). He knew that he was safe in the Father's will, and that they could not kill him until his hour had come.

God in his mercy can and does answer "emergency prayers," but he prefers that we be in constant communion with him. (In fact, if we seek to live in his will, we may have fewer emergencies!) If prayer is an interruption to our lives, then something is wrong.

The fact that we sustain an attitude of prayer does not mean we avoid regular times of prayer. It is the regular occasion of prayer that makes possible the constant attitude of prayer. We do not enjoy Thanksgiving dinners or holiday feasts at every meal, but we are able to enjoy those special times because we have eaten our regular meals three times a day. We begin the day with prayer; we pray at mealtime; we lift prayers to God during the day as the Spirit prompts us; we close the day in prayer. Like our breathing, our praying becomes so much a part of our lives that we are often not conscious of it.

4. *The glory of God should be our primary concern.* "Father, the hour has come; glorify Thy Son, that the Son may glorify Thee."

The word "glory" is used in one form or another eight times in this prayer. What does it mean?

In the Old Testament, the Hebrew word translated "glory" means "weight, that which is important and honorable." (Paul's phrase "an eternal weight of glory" in 2 Corinthians 4:17 carries this idea.) In the New Testament, the Greek word translated "glory" means "opinion, fame." Theologians tell us that the "glory of God" is the sum total of all that he is, the manifestation of his character. The glory of God is not an attribute of God, but rather is an attribute of all his attributes! He is glorious in wisdom and power, glorious in his mighty works, and glorious in the grace he bestows upon us.

You have probably noticed that "The Lord's Prayer" teaches us to put God's concerns before our own. We pray "Hallowed be Thy Name, Thy kingdom come, Thy will be done" before we bring up our own needs—daily bread, forgiveness, and protection from sin. When our praying centers on the glory of God, we see our needs and requests in proper perspective. Matters that seemed so important have a tendency to shrink to their proper size when measured by the glory of God.

Whatever we pray about, in the will of God and for the glory of God, will be granted by our heavenly Father. When we are available to bring glory to God "on the earth" (v. 4), then God is available to provide what we need.

Was Jesus praying selfishly when he said, "Glorify Thy Son"? No, he was not. To begin with, he had shared that glory with the Father "before the world was" (v. 5). When

31

he came to earth in his body of flesh, he veiled that glory. Peter, James, and John saw it on the Mount of Transfiguration (Matt. 17:1–8; John 1:14), but it was not revealed to anyone else. When our Lord asked the Father to glorify him, he was only requesting the return of that which was already his.

But something more is involved. The glorification of Jesus Christ meant the completion of the great work of salvation. In this prayer, Jesus spoke as though his work on the cross were already finished. "I glorified Thee on the earth, having accomplished the work which Thou hast given me to do" (v. 4). If Jesus Christ had not been glorified, there could be no salvation for sinners today. The Holy Spirit would not have been given. There would be no church, no New Testament, no Christian life. While our Lord did pray for himself, it was not a selfish prayer, for he also had us in mind. And, after all, it cost him his life on the cross for this prayer to be answered. By no stretch of the imagination could you call it selfish.

God answered the prayer of his Son. "The God of Abraham, Isaac, and Jacob, the God of our fathers, has glorified His Servant Jesus. . . ." (Acts 3:13). In 1 Peter 1:21 we are told that the Father "raised Him from the dead and gave Him glory. . . ." *There is a glorified Man in heaven today!* In Jesus Christ, deity and humanity share glory. This assures us that one day *we* shall share God's glory, for "we shall be like Him, because we shall see Him just as He is" (1 John 3:2).

Jesus Christ has already given his church the glory (v. 22). The tense of the verb in Romans 8:30 has always astounded me: "whom He justified, these He also glorified." We are just as much glorified as we are justified, *but the glory has not yet been revealed.* All of creation, now travailing because of sin, is eagerly awaiting "the revealing of the sons of God" (Rom. 8:19), for only then will creation be set free to enjoy "the freedom of the glory of the children of God" (Rom. 8:21).

"If God answers this request," we should ask ourselves, "will it bring him glory? And what will this answer look like when Jesus comes again?" I have discovered that testing my prayers by the glory of God is a good way to detect requests that are selfish and shortsighted.

5. *We must pray in faith.*

Suppose the Master had looked at his situation through human eyes alone. Could he have prayed as he did? No, it would have been impossible.

Suppose he looked back on his years of ministry and evaluated that ministry from a human point of view. It would have looked like failure. He had very few followers, and his own nation had rejected him. Humanly speaking, his work had failed. Yet he prayed, "I glorified Thee on the earth, having accomplished the work which Thou hast given me to do" (v. 4). By faith, he would be that "grain of wheat" planted in the ground, and he would produce much fruit (John 12:24).

Or, suppose he had looked around. What would he have seen? A small band of men, all of whom would fail him in one way or another. Peter would deny him three times. At that very hour, Judas was bargaining with the Jewish council and selling the Master like a common slave. Peter, James, and John would go to sleep in the Garden when they should be encouraging their Lord. And all of the men would forsake him and flee.

Yet by faith, Jesus prayed, "I have been glorified in them" (v. 10). By faith, he prayed for them as they would be sent into the world to share the gospel message. In spite of their past failures, *these men would succeed!* "I do not ask in behalf of these alone," he said to the Father, "but for those also who believe in Me through their word" (v. 20). These weak men would invade a world that hated them and bring many to the feet of the Savior. Jesus saw all of this by faith.

If our Lord had looked ahead, he would have seen arrest, conviction, and death on a cross. Humanly speaking, it was defeat; but by faith, he saw it as it really was—victory! He said to Andrew and Philip, "The hour has come for the Son of Man to be glorified" (John 12:23). *Glorified!* We would have said *crucified.* But he looked beyond the cross to the glory that would come. "Who for the joy set before Him endured the cross, despising the shame, and has sat down at the right hand of the throne of God" (Heb. 12:2).

When we pray by faith, we start seeing things from the divine perspective. Faith enables us to see the invisible. Faith treats as present and accomplished that which God will do in the future. "For we walk by faith, not by sight" (2 Cor. 5:7).

In my own prayer life, God is constantly seeking to bring me back to these fundamentals. It is easy for me to get detoured by some external thing, and my Father has to remind me that effective praying must come from the heart. I must repeatedly examine my relationship to the Father to make sure I am in his will, and that I *want* to be in his will ("doing the will of God from the heart," Eph. 6:6). I must examine my motives: Am I praying so that the Father will be glorified or so that I might have my own comfortable way? Am I praying by faith, basing my requests on his Word?

Perhaps all of this seems to make praying appear very complex and difficult. Really, it is not. *True prayer is the by-product of our personal "love relationship" with the Father.* "He who has My commandments and keeps them, he it is who loves Me; and he who loves Me shall be loved by My Father, and I will love him, and will disclose Myself to him" (John 14:21).

THREE REMARKABLE GIFTS

Even as Thou gavest Him authority over all mankind, that to all whom Thou hast given Him, He may give eternal life. And this is eternal life, that they may know Thee, the only true God, and Jesus Christ whom Thou hast sent.

—John 17:2–3

The idea of *giving* is important in this prayer—in fact, in all of the Gospel of John. "Give" in one form or another is used seventeen times in our Lord's prayer and seventy-six times in the Gospel of John.

Learning to give, and to receive, is an important part of life. John Donne was right: "No man is an island. . . ." We depend on each other and we need each other. Most of all, we need God. Apart from the generous giving of our gracious God, we would have nothing. "A man can receive nothing," said John the Baptist, "unless it has been given him from heaven" (John 3:27).

Three remarkable gifts are mentioned in John 17:2. An understanding of these gifts will help us better understand God's great plan of salvation and how we fit into it.

1. *The Father gave the Son authority.*

Here we are introduced to the mysterious inner workings of the Trinity, the plans that were made "before the world was" (v. 5). It was decreed that, because the Son would suffer and die, he would be granted authority to give eternal life to those who would trust him. (As we shall see later, those who trust him are also the Father's gift to the Son.) It was on the basis of this authority that Jesus prayed to be glorified. Unless he was glorified, he could not share the gift of eternal life. That is why verse 2 begins with "even as." The authority and the glory go together.

Authority is the right to act, to exercise power. If a burglar carrying a gun enters my house, he has power but no authority. If a policeman shows up carrying a gun, he has both power and authority. But somebody had to give that policeman the authority to act. "By what authority are You doing these things," the Jewish leaders asked Jesus, "and who gave You this authority?" (Matt. 21:23).

God the Father gave Jesus Christ the authority to do what he did on earth. (Of course, as the eternal Son in heaven our Lord possessed all the authority of the Godhead. It is his ministry on earth that we are considering.) To begin with, the Father gave the Son the authority to die and be raised again. "For this reason the Father loves Me, because I lay down My life that I may take it again. No one has taken it away from Me, but I lay it down on My own initiative. I have authority to lay it down, and I have authority to take it up again. This commandment I received from My Father" (John 10:17–18).

The death of Christ was not an accident; it was an appointment. It was not a mistake; it was planned. It was not martyrdom or suicide. It was the willing offering of the Son of God on the cross for the sins of the world. Jesus Christ is the only one the Father has authorized to be the Savior of the world. Anyone else who claims this authority is a liar.

The Father also gave the Son the authority to judge. "For just as the Father has life in Himself, even so He gave to the Son also to have life in Himself; and He gave Him authority to execute judgment, because He is the Son of Man" (John 5:26–27). He is both Savior and Judge, for the two go together. Those who will not receive him as Savior must face him as Judge. The fact that Jesus ministered in a human body here on earth helps to qualify him as Judge. No man can ever say, "You don't know what we experienced!" Our Lord knows man because he is the Son of man.

When our Lord ascended to heaven to return to the Father, he said to his followers: "All authority has been given to Me in heaven and on earth" (Matt. 28:18). This includes the authority to give eternal life.

Our Lord's authority extends over "all mankind," or, as the original Greek reads, "all flesh." Man is simply "flesh" and as such has no lasting glory. "For all flesh is like grass, and all its glory like the flower of grass" (1 Peter 1:24, quoted from Isaiah 40:6). The first mention in the Bible of "all flesh" is significant: "And God looked on the earth, and behold it was corrupt; for all flesh had corrupted their way upon the earth" (Gen. 6:12). Man is only flesh, and the glory of flesh does not last.

In his grace and love, the Lord Jesus Christ took upon himself "the likeness of sinful flesh" (Rom. 8:3). He was truly human, yet he was without sin. He entered into our world of "flesh" that he might bring us into the world of "spirit." His association with human nature was not temporary; it was permanent. He took a human body to heaven, and there it shares the eternal glory of God.

2. *The Father gives people to the Son.*

Jesus Christ has the authority to give eternal life, but he does not give this precious gift to everybody. He gives eternal life to those whom the Father has given to him. At least four times in this prayer Jesus identifies the saved as those who have been given to him by the Father.

Again, we are entering into the mysteries of the eternal arrangement made by the glorious Trinity before the creation of the world. Theologians call this the doctrine of "divine election." God the Father has decreed that God the Son shall receive "a people"—the church—because of his completed work on the cross. God the Son is the Father's love gift to a lost world, but the church is the Father's love gift to his beloved Son.

The Scriptures affirm that all three Persons in the Godhead are involved in our salvation. This is a part of the eternal covenant made within the Godhead. God's plan of salvation was not an afterthought. "This Man [Jesus], delivered up by the predetermined plan and foreknowledge of God, you nailed to a cross by the hand of godless men and put Him to death" (Acts 2:23). "For He was foreknown before the foundation of the world, but has appeared in these last times for the sake of you" (1 Peter 1:20).

Two lines of truth seem to run parallel in the Bible: one, that God has chosen his "elect" from eternity, and two, that these "elect" have made a responsible decision to trust Christ. "All that the Father gives Me shall come to Me [that's divine election], and the one who comes to Me [that's human responsibility] I will certainly not cast out" (John 6:37). If we deny divine election, then we make salvation the work of man. If we deny human responsibility, then we make man *less than* man, a mere robot fulfilling the eternal plan of God. "Salvation is from the LORD" (Jonah 2:9) expresses divine sovereignty. "Seek the LORD while He may be found" (Isa. 55:6) expresses human responsibility. A paradox? Yes. A mystery? To be sure! An impossibility? No! One of my professors at seminary said, "Try to explain divine election, and you may lose your mind. Try to explain it away, and you may lose your soul." Truth is not always at one extreme or the other. Sometimes truth is found at that subtle point of paradox where two opposites meet. At any rate, it is not necessary for a lost sinner to comprehend the mysteries of divine election in order to be saved. He knows that God loves him (John 3:16) and that God is not willing that any should perish (2 Peter 3:9). He knows that the promise of salvation is for "everyone who calls on the name of the Lord" (Acts 2:21). If he calls, God will answer him and save him.

We have already noted that all three Persons in the Godhead are involved in our salvation. Perhaps this truth can help us better understand God's part and our part in the miracle of salvation.

As far as God the Father is concerned, I was saved when he chose me in Christ before the foundation of the world (Eph. 1:4). Of course, I knew nothing about that choice. As far as God the Son is concerned, I was saved when he died for me on the cross, for he died for the sins of the whole world (1 John 2:2). This is the message of the gospel, the Good News that sinners can be saved. I had known that Good News since childhood, but it never really struck home until one night at the Youth for Christ rally. I heard the evangelist as he preached the gospel, and I trusted Jesus Christ and was saved. So, as far as the Holy Spirit is concerned, I was saved that May night in 1945 when I responded to the Spirit's call.

Now, to emphasize the ministry of one member of the Godhead to the neglect of the others would be wrong. Or to so emphasize God's part to the minimizing of man's part would also be wrong. Paul kept all of these things in balance when he wrote: "But we should always give thanks to God for you, brethren beloved by the Lord, because God has chosen you from the beginning for salvation through sanctification by the Spirit and faith in the truth. And it was for this He called you through our gospel, that you may gain the glory of our Lord Jesus Christ" (2 Thess. 2:13–14).

If I did not believe that God was working out his perfect plan in this world, I would stop ministering. The fact that God has an elect people in this world is, to me, a great encouragement for ministry, whether it is preaching, writing, witnessing, or praying. When Paul became discouraged in the polluted city of Corinth, the Lord reassured him: "Do not be afraid any longer, but go on speaking and do not be silent; for I am with you, for I have many people in this city" (Acts 18:9–10). Jesus called these people "those whom Thou hast given Me."

Of course, the doctrine of election is a great blow to man's pride. It is unfortunate when some personal workers and evangelists give lost sinners the impression that the sinner is doing God a favor by trusting his Son. Or sometimes they convey the idea that God is paralyzed unless the lost sinner does something to help himself get saved. The sinner chooses—and then discovers that he has been chosen! He believes—and then finds out that his faith and repentance were God's gift (Acts 11:18). He cannot explain it, but he can enjoy it; and he gladly affirms with Jonah, "Salvation is from the LORD!"

There are five special blessings that belong to those who have been given to the Son by the Father:

a. *Eternal life* (v. 2). We will study this gift in detail in the last part of this chapter.
b. *The knowledge of the Father* (vv. 6–7). The lost world does not know God (v. 25). Only those who have been

given by the Father to the Son know him. To "know his name" means to know his person, to understand his nature. God's children do not just know *about* the Father; they know the Father personally.

c. *Christ's intercession on their behalf* (v. 9). When he was on earth, Christ prayed for his disciples. Today he is praying for all believers. This is part of his great ministry as our High Priest in heaven. (See Rom. 8:34; Heb. 7:25; 9:24.)

d. *Divine protection in this world* (vv. 11–12). This involves the physical and spiritual well-being of God's people. It also involves their spiritual unity in Christ. God guards his own.

e. *Eternal glory* (v. 24). This is our assurance of heaven. No one will be in heaven who has not first of all been given to Jesus Christ.

How important it is to know that we have been given to Christ! No wonder Peter wrote, "Therefore, my brothers, be all the more eager to make your calling and election sure" (2 Peter 1:10 NIV). In this present era of "easy believism" and shallow evangelism, there are doubtless many professed Christians who have never been converted at all. A well-known Christian leader told me that he believed half of the people in our churches were not born again. Paul warned the members of his church at Corinth, "Test yourselves to see if you are in the faith; examine yourselves!" (2 Cor. 13:5).

3. *The Son gives eternal life to those who are given to him.* The word "life" is used thirty-six times in John's Gospel. In fact, John wrote his Gospel so that sinners might trust Christ and receive eternal life (John 20:31). There is no question that eternal life is the greatest gift anyone could ever receive.

But what is "eternal life"? Certainly it is more than *extended* life—living forever—because even the lost will live forever, but separated from God. "And these will pay the penalty of eternal destruction, away from the presence of the Lord and from the glory of His power" (2 Thess. 1:9). Eternal life is not endless time; it is God's own life shared with us now. It is not a quantity of time but a quality of experience. In fact, eternal life cannot be affected by time. Like the eternal God who gives eternal life, the gift is beyond time and outside time. When you have eternal life, you have God's own life here and now—and forever.

The British expositor, Dr. G. Campbell Morgan, has pointed out that John describes for his readers all the essentials for life. For example, there can be no life without *light*. "In Him [Christ] was life; and the life was the light of men" (John 1:4). Nor can there be life without *breath*. "He breathed on them, and said to them, 'Receive the Holy Spirit'" (John 20:22; and see also the Holy Spirit as "wind" in John 3:8). *Water* is another essential for life: "Whoever drinks of the water that I shall give him shall never thirst; but the water that I shall give him shall become in him a well of water springing up to eternal life" (John 4:14). A fourth essential for life is *food*, and Jesus said, "I am the bread of life" (John 6:35).

Of course, this gift of eternal life comes through what Jesus called "being born again" (John 3:1–21). Our first birth was a physical birth, but the second birth that brings salvation is a spiritual birth. Our first birth made us sons of Adam and therefore sinners; our second birth makes us the sons and daughters of God and forever settles the problem of sin.

In John 17:3, our Lord explained eternal life in terms of "knowing God." But we must not interpret this to mean a mere intellectual acquaintance with God. Knowing *about* God is not the same as *knowing* God personally. The history of the Greek word translated "know" indicates that the word means "to know with experience." It is not merely an opinion or a mental acceptance. To know something or someone means to grasp the full reality of it or him, to penetrate into the very nature of the object or person. In the Old Testament, the Hebrew word for "to know" also described the intimate relationship between man and wife (Gen. 4:1, 25), and this same meaning is carried over into the New Testament (Matt. 1:25; Luke 1:34).

How can a sinner get to know God in this intimate, personal, saving way? *Only through Jesus Christ.* The apostle Philip said, "Lord, show us the Father, and it is enough for us." Jesus replied, "Have I been so long with you, and yet you have not come to know Me, Philip? He who has seen Me has seen the Father" (John 14:8–9). It is only when we yield to Jesus Christ that we get to know the Father in the experience of eternal life.

Consider the characteristics of this gift of eternal life. Certainly it is the most *expensive* gift ever given, for it cost Jesus Christ his life. It is an *eternal* gift. Unlike most of the gifts we receive, which either break or wear out, eternal life gets better and better as the years move on. Eternal life is an *essential* gift—everybody needs it. If you had to give one gift to everybody in the world, what would it be? Not everyone can read books; not everyone wears the same kind of clothing; not everybody needs money; tastes in food differ from one place to another. The only gift that is suitable for everybody is eternal life, for everybody needs it.

Eternal life is an *expressive* gift: "God so loved the world that He gave. . . ." (John 3:16). Some gifts are given out of obligation or guilt, or even pride; but eternal life is given as the expression of the Father's great love for us.

But eternal life is an *exclusive* gift. Only those receive eternal life who have been given to the Son by the Father. There is only one true God; there is only one Savior. Only Jesus Christ has the authority to give eternal life to those who trust him. How tragic it is when lost sinners refuse to accept this free gift! "And you are unwilling to come to Me, that you may have life" (John 5:40).

The subject of eternal life is so vast that we could go on for many more pages, but I want to close with this observation: When people possess eternal life, you can tell it by their everyday life. When a person says, "I know God!" then he ought to back up that profession with practice. For one thing, he will be *obedient to God's will.* "The one who says, 'I have come to know Him,' and does not keep His commandments, is a liar, and the truth is not in him" (1 John 2:4). He will also practice *love for the brethren.* "The one who does not love does not know God, for God is love" (1 John 4:8). Saying that we know God carries tremendous responsibilities.

The opposite of eternal life is eternal death, the second death, the lake of fire (Rev. 20:11–15). Eternal life means knowing God; eternal death means separation from God. "For God did not send the Son into the world to judge the world, but that the world should be saved through Him" (John 3:17).

Have you received the gift of eternal life?

Are you sharing the Good News of this gift with others?

WHAT HAPPENED
"BEFORE THE WORLD WAS"

I glorified Thee on the earth, having accomplished
the work which Thou hast given Me to do. And now,
glorify Thou Me together with Thyself, Father, with
the glory which I ever had with Thee before the world
was.

—John 17:4–5

What is the earliest recollection that you can un-
earth from the deep mine of your memory? I
have a faint remembrance of my mother going
to the hospital for surgery and an aunt coming to care for
us children, but the picture is quite dim.

The oldest written text the historian can lay his hands
on is dated about 3500 B.C. It is found on some clay tablets
unearthed in Iraq in 1952.

But the Bible takes us back beyond time and into eternity. Why? Because we can never really understand what is
going on "in time" unless we know what happened "before

the world was." As Dr. A. T. Pierson used to say, "History is His story." A modern novelist has affirmed that "everything is accident," but the Christian knows better. Everything is *appointment*. If you and I did not believe that God was on his throne, working out his perfect will, we would sink in the storms of life. The hymn writer William Cowper expressed it perfectly:

> *God moves in a mysterious way*
> *His wonders to perform;*
> *He plants His footsteps in the sea*
> *And rides upon the storm.*
> *Deep in unfathomable mines*
> *Of never-failing skill*
> *He treasures up His bright designs*
> *And works His sovereign will.*

Modern self-made man with his egotistical emphasis on "do-it-my-way-living" wants nothing to do with a sovereign God. To be sure, the sovereignty of God in no way eliminates human responsibility or man's moral freedom; but it does mean that God *rules*, and when he is not permitted to rule, that he *overrules*.

All of which takes us back to our Lord's statement "before the world was." Let's try to answer, from the Scriptures, the important question: What was going on "before the world was"? Several facts emerge to help us discover the answer.

1. *Jesus existed as eternal God.*

Of course, all three members of the Godhead existed, but our special focus of attention in John 17 is the Lord Jesus Christ. In fact, this is the focus of John's Gospel: "that you may believe that Jesus is the Christ, the Son of God; and that believing you may have life in His name" (John 20:31). We noted in chapter 1 the evidences in John 17 alone that prove that Jesus Christ is eternal God.

46

The Gospel of John opens with a declaration of the deity of Christ: "In the beginning was the Word, and the Word was with God, and the Word was God. He was in the beginning with God" (John 1:1–2).

It is worth noting that six different persons in John's Gospel bear witness that Jesus is the Son of God: John the Baptist (1:34), Nathanael (1:49), Peter (6:69), the healed blind man (9:35–38), Martha (11:27), and Thomas (20:28). The Samaritans called him "the Savior of the world" (4:42), a title that could only belong to deity. Our Lord himself affirmed his eternality in John 8:58: "Truly, truly, I say to you, before Abraham was born, I AM." The people attempted to stone him for this statement because they knew what it meant: "For a good work we do not stone You, but for blasphemy; and because You, being a man, make Yourself out to be God" (John 10:33).

The fact that Jesus Christ existed before the creation of the world helps us to understand the necessity for the virgin birth (Isa. 7:14; Matt. 1:18–25; Luke 1:26–38). Every baby born into this world is a new person who has never existed before. But Jesus Christ existed before the world was, before there were people. Therefore, when he was to take upon himself a human body, it could not have been through the normal process of human reproduction. After all, Jesus existed before his mother was born! Joseph was not the biological father of Jesus Christ, though he certainly was the legal father according to the Jewish records. Jesus Christ was conceived by the Holy Spirit in the womb of Mary, for this is the way a preexisting person must come into the world as a human.

In other words, Jesus existed from eternity in heaven having a Father and no mother; but he came into the world having an earthly mother but no earthly biological father.

"Before the world was" the Trinity existed in timeless, dateless communion. The hymn writer Frederick Faber has expressed it this way:

> *Timeless, spaceless, single, lonely,*
> *Yet sublimely Three,*
> *You are grandly, always, only*
> *God in Unity!*
> *Lone in grandeur, lone in glory,*
> *Who shall tell Thy wondrous story*
> *Awful Trinity?*

The fact defies explanation and comprehension; yet it is true. If it is not true, then Jesus Christ lied, the Bible is fantasy, and our universe is an accidental conglomerate of electrical particles that came out of nowhere.

2. *Jesus shared the Father's glory.*

He stated this in verse 5: "And now, glorify Thou Me together with Thyself, Father, with the glory which I ever had with Thee before the world was." Hebrews 1:3 states it: "And He is the radiance of His [the Father's] glory and the exact representation of His nature." The apostle John testified: "And the Word became flesh, and dwelt among us, and we beheld His glory, glory as of the only begotten from the Father, full of grace and truth" (John 1:14).

As we have seen, the glory of God is the sum total of all that he is, the expression of his character. It is the manifestation of all that he is in himself, his marvelous attributes. We have a difficult time grasping the concept of God's glory because there is nothing like it on earth. While it is true that "the heavens are telling of the glory of God" (Ps. 19:1), it is also true that sin has put God's creation into bondage and robbed God of glory (Rom. 8:18–25). Psalm 19 makes special mention of the sun as an illustration of God's glory, and perhaps that is the closest we can come to finding a picture. Just as the rays of the sun cannot be separated from the sun itself, so Jesus Christ cannot be separated from God, because he is God.

The amazing thing is this: Those who have trusted Jesus Christ as their Savior possess this glory now (John 17:22) and will see God's glory and share it in heaven one day (John 17:24). God does not need people or anything else in order to be glorious. He is glorious in himself and eternally self-sufficient. Yet in his grace, he deigned to share his glory with sinful man! And Jesus Christ was willing to lay aside his glory to die so that sinners, all of whom have fallen short of God's glory (Rom. 3:23), might receive that glory.

3. *Jesus was beloved of the Father.*

He stated this in verse 24: "for Thou didst love Me before the foundation of the world." "God is love" (1 John 4:8). Before God poured his love out on mankind, the Persons of the Godhead expressed their perfect love to one another in a glorious communion. The Scriptures especially point out the Father's love for the Son.

When Jesus was baptized, the Father affirmed his love: "This is My beloved Son, in whom I am well-pleased" (Matt. 3:17). This was the Father's "heavenly seal of approval" on the life Jesus had lived as a boy, youth, and young man in Nazareth. From our Lord's twelfth year until his thirtieth year, we have no record of what he said or did, except that he was in subjection to Mary and Joseph and that he developed as any normal child (Luke 2:51–52). But the Father made it clear at the baptism that the Son had lived a perfect life, well-pleasing to the Father.

The Father reaffirmed his love when Jesus was transfigured on the mountain: "This is My beloved Son, with whom I am well-pleased; hear Him!" (Matt. 17:5). Moses and Elijah were with Jesus on the mount, yet the Father did not give special attention to them. Peter, James, and John were also there, but no voice of approval was addressed to them. It was the Son, Jesus Christ, who was singled out as the recipient of the Father's special love and approval. This must have been a great encouragement to the Savior as he faced the cross.

The prophets bore witness to the Father's love for the Son. "Behold, My Servant whom I have chosen; My Beloved in whom My soul is well-pleased" (Matt. 12:18, quoted from Isa. 42:1).

Jesus alluded to the Father's love in his parable about the wicked men and the vineyard (Luke 20:9–18). "And the owner of the vineyard said, 'What shall I do? I will send my beloved son; perhaps they will respect him'" (v. 13).

The apostle Paul also affirms this eternal love of the Father for the Son: "giving thanks to the Father, who has qualified us to share in the inheritance of the saints in light. For He delivered us from the domain of darkness, and transferred us to the kingdom of His beloved Son"—literally "the Son of His love" (Col. 1:12–13).

It is impossible for the human mind to grasp the concept of eternity. We cannot imagine timelessness and spacelessness. "Time" and "place" help to keep order in our lives. Yet the Father and the Son and the Spirit existed eternally, sharing an eternal love. If we, in this brief span of time that we call "life," can learn to love deeply the people that we do, and if we, with our sins, can grow in our love for others, just think of what kind of perfect, timeless, uninterrupted, unchanging love the Father and the Son and the Spirit enjoyed.

And think of what it meant when the Son left the bosom of the Father and came to earth to be hated! John 3:16, familiar as it is, takes on new depth of meaning when you try to comprehend the eternal love of the Father for the Son.

4. *The Father established his eternal purpose.*

"This was in accordance with the eternal purpose which He [the Father] carried out in Christ Jesus our Lord" (Eph. 3:11). This purpose is further described in Ephesians 1:10–12: "with a view to an administration suitable to the fullness of the times, that is, the summing up of all things in Christ, things in the heavens and things upon the earth. In

Him also we have obtained an inheritance, having been pre-destined according to His purpose who works all things after the counsel of His will, to the end that we who were the first to hope in Christ should be to the praise of His glory."

That God has an "eternal purpose" for all things is both scriptural and logical. If God is God at all, he is sovereign. He cannot work independently of his own nature, for then he would cease to be God, something that is impossible. He is a wise God; therefore, his eternal purpose is a wise one. He is a powerful God; therefore, he is able to accomplish what he purposes. He is a loving God; therefore, what he purposes will manifest his love. He is an unchanging God; therefore, his purpose is unchanging.

God's ultimate purpose is to bring glory to his name: "to the praise of the glory of His grace . . . to the praise of His glory . . . to the praise of His glory. . . ." (Eph. 1:6, 12, 14). He will do this by uniting "all things in Christ" (Eph. 1:10). Today sin is dividing and destroying, but when God wraps up history all things will unite in Christ and bring glory to God.

Words like "predestination" and "election" frighten some people and are greatly misunderstood by others. "If God has an eternal purpose, then why bother to do anything?" some people ask. "Why pray? Why send out missionaries? After all, God will certainly achieve his purpose!"

But not without us! God has ordained (and this is amazing) that his purposes shall be fulfilled in and through his church. Why pray? Because prayer is one of God's ordained ways to accomplish his will in us and through us. Why send out missionaries? Because he has commanded us to carry the gospel to the ends of the earth, and our obedience is part of his ordained plan. God's eternal purpose, established "before the world was," is not an excuse for carelessness and disobedience. It is one of our greatest encouragements to obedience and service.

51

God's eternal purpose is not fatalism. Rather, it is the perfect plan of a loving Father, and our Father loves us too much to harm us. He is too wise to make mistakes. "The counsel of the LORD stands forever, the plans of His heart from generation to generation" (Ps. 33:11). Note that important phrase: "the plans of His heart. . . ."

Please keep in mind that a part of God's eternal plan is the fact that man shall have moral freedom. Divine sovereignty and human responsibility do not conflict with or contradict each other; they are friends, not enemies. You and I cannot fathom this because we are creatures of time with minds incapable of understanding God's vast purpose. *But this does not keep us from believing it and acting upon it.* The greatest Christian theologian who ever lived wrote, "Oh, the depth of the riches both of the wisdom and knowledge of God! How unsearchable are His judgments and unfathomable His ways!" (Rom. 11:33). If the apostle Paul admitted that he was over his head when he thought about God's eternal plan, where does that leave you and me?

God's eternal plan is not a discouragement to prayer, but an encouragement. At least, the early church found it so. Read the prayer recorded in Acts 4:24–31, and note their faith in God's sovereignty: "to do whatever Thy hand and Thy purpose predestined to occur" (Acts 4:28). Nor did faith in God's eternal purpose hinder their preaching of the gospel: "this Man, delivered up by the predetermined plan and foreknowledge of God, you nailed to a cross. . . ." (Acts 2:23). Calvary was not a mistake or an accident; it was part of God's eternal plan.

"But why did God plan it this way?" some may ask. Because his plan is the best. God cannot ordain less than the very best. There are some things about God's plan that we may not understand, but we agree with our Lord's affirmation of faith in Matthew 11:26: "Yes, Father, for thus it was well-pleasing in Thy sight." And if any of us gets the idea that God needed our help as consultants, we had better listen again to Paul: "For who has known the mind of the Lord, or who became His counselor?" (Rom. 11:34). God did not need our help in framing his great plan, nor does he need our criticism of it. But he does want to share with us the privilege of working out his plan in this world. Is God's plan going to succeed? Of course it is! "Truly I have spoken; truly I will bring it to pass. I have planned it, surely I will do it" (Isa. 46:11). It is because of this eternal purpose that "God causes all things to work together for good to those who love God. . . ." (Rom. 8:28).

5. *The Father elected people to be saved.*

This, of course, is a part of God's eternal plan: "Just as He chose us in Him [Christ] before the foundation of the world. . . ." (Eph. 1:4); "who has saved us, and called us with a holy calling, not according to our works, but according to His own purpose and grace which was granted us in Christ Jesus from all eternity" (2 Tim. 1:9); "in the hope of eternal life, which God who cannot lie, promised long ages ago [literally, before times eternal]" (Titus 1:2).

God did not choose any to be saved because of their good works or personal merit. Salvation is wholly by grace (Eph. 2:8–9). God's sovereign choice is based upon his own divine purpose. For that matter, God does not have to save *any* sinner! His electing grace is the expression of his eternal love. To be sure, there are mysteries here that we cannot explain, and it does not promote practical godliness to debate them. "The secret things belong to the LORD our God, but the things revealed belong to us and to our sons forever. . . ." (Deut. 29:29).

It is important to remember that divine sovereignty does not negate human responsibility. What God had ordained in eternity must be worked out in time. We may be "chosen . . . from the beginning for salvation," but we are also called through the human instrumentality of the preaching of the gospel (2 Thess. 2:13–14). The same God who ordains the end (the salvation of lost sinners) also ordains the means to the end; and that is where prayer, witnessing, good works, and the exercise of the means of grace all come in.

6. *The Son covenanted to die for sinners.* Calvary was not a divine afterthought or a stopgap measure devised by a frustrated God who was caught unawares. Calvary was part of God's eternal purpose. In his powerful sermon at Pentecost, Peter affirmed that Jesus was "delivered up by the predetermined plan and foreknowledge of God" (Acts 2:23). Our Lord himself said to his disciples, "For indeed, the Son of Man is going as it has been determined. . . ." (Luke 22:22). The Lamb was "foreknown before the foundation of the world" (1 Peter 1:20).

When our Lord uttered the prayer recorded in John 17, he looked upon the cross as a completed ministry. "I glorified Thee on the earth, having accomplished the work which Thou hast given Me to do." What kind of work was this?

To begin with, it was *an assigned work*. God the Father gave the Son the assignment. It was a part of the "eternal covenant" (Heb. 13:20–21) that the Son should die for the sins of the world. While each Person in the Godhead is equal to each of the other Persons, it is still true that each Person has an assigned ministry in the plan of salvation. According to Ephesians 1:1–14, we are chosen by the Father, purchased by the Son, and sealed by the Spirit. We are "chosen according to the foreknowledge of God the Father, by the sanctifying work of the Spirit, that you may obey Jesus Christ and be sprinkled with His blood. . . ." (1 Peter 1:1–2).

It is interesting to trace in the Gospels the stages in our Lord's revelation of this assigned work. When the Savior was born, his testimony was, "Behold, I have come . . . to do Thy will, O God" (Heb. 10:7). When he was twelve years old, Jesus said to Mary and Joseph when they found him in the temple, "Why is it that you were looking for

Me? Did you not know that I had to be in My Father's house?" [literally, "in the affairs of My Father"].

Jesus told his disciples, "My food is to do the will of Him who sent Me, and to accomplish His work" (John 4:34). "For I have come down from heaven, not to do My own will, but the will of Him who sent Me" (John 6:38). When he voluntarily yielded his life on the cross, he shouted, "It is finished!" (John 19:30).

Nobody but Jesus Christ could have accepted this assignment and completed it successfully. The great work of salvation demanded the perfect sacrifice, the spotless Lamb of God. In his love for us, Jesus Christ accepted the assignment and brought it to a successful conclusion.

In other words, the work that he did is *a finished work.* Nothing need be added to it, and certainly nothing dare be taken from it. When our Lord died on the cross, the veil of the temple was torn from top to bottom (Matt. 27:51). This announced the end of the Mosaic law, "for the Law made nothing perfect" (Heb. 7:19). It also announced the end of the Jewish priesthood, for the priesthood could make no sinner perfect before God (Heb. 7:11). It declared the end of the sacrificial system, for the sacrifices could make no man perfect (Heb. 9:9 and 10:1).

Our Lord finished the work of redemption on the cross, returned to heaven, and *sat down.* The Old Testament priests did not sit down in the sanctuary, for their work was never finished. "But He [Jesus], having offered one sacrifice for sins for all time, sat down at the right hand of God" (Heb. 10:12). "For by one offering He has perfected for all time those who are sanctified" (Heb. 10:14). That phrase "for all time" is in the original Greek "perpetually, continually, forever."

Since the work of redemption is finished, all that sinners need to do is believe it and accept it for themselves.

His work was an assigned work and a finished work; but it is also *a glorious work.* "I glorified Thee on the earth, having accomplished the work which Thou hast given Me to do." Of course, everything that Jesus did was glorious. Even the common activities of life, like the breaking of bread or the cuddling of a baby, had the touch of glory about them.

When our Lord was born in Bethlehem, the angels announced the event to the shepherds, "and the glory of the Lord shone around them" (Luke 2:9). "We beheld His glory," confessed John (John 1:14). Even our Lord's death on the cross was seen in the light of God's glory: "The hour has come for the Son of Man to be glorified" (John 12:23).

Sin has robbed man of God's glory, "for all have sinned and fall short of the glory of God" (Rom. 3:23). The glory of man—flesh—does not last. "All flesh is like grass, and all its glory like the flower of grass" (1 Peter 1:24). Great men and women come and go, and yesterday's heroes are today's forgotten people. The glory of man is always in the past tense: the glory that was Rome, the glory that was Greece.

The purpose of redemption is the glory of God. There are many blessed by-products of redemption, like the transforming of lives and the restoring of homes. All of this has as its ultimate goal the glory of God. Our Lord did many mighty works on this earth, and all of them revealed God's glory (John 2:11). But the greatest and most glorious work he did was the finished work of salvation on the cross. This glorious work was planned before the foundation of the world.

Yes, there are some profound truths in these verses. When we, with human minds and hearts, begin to think and meditate on what happened "before the world was," we soon find ourselves beyond our limit. These truths were not given so that we might debate, but that we might surrender and worship. It is not a big head, but a burning heart, that proves we have grasped something of the meaning of God's eternal plan.

THE DYNAMICS OF DISCIPLESHIP

I manifested Thy name to the men whom Thou gavest Me out of the world; Thine they were, and Thou gavest them to Me, and they have kept Thy word. Now they have come to know that everything Thou hast given Me is from Thee; for the words which Thou gavest Me I have given to them; and they received them, and truly understood that I came forth from Thee, and they believed that Thou didst send me.

—John 17:6–8

Discipleship is a popular topic in the church these days. It seems like just about everybody is discipling somebody. The word that is translated "disciple" in our English New Testament is used 264 times, and it is found *exclusively* in the four Gospels and in Acts. Nowhere in the Epistles are the believers called "disciples," although the verb "to disciple" is found in eighteen places in the Epistles and the Book of Revelation.

In New Testament days, a "disciple" was someone who bound himself to a teacher in order to learn both the theory and the practice of some subject or trade. Perhaps our closest modern equivalent would be "apprentice." A true disciple was not simply a student who learned from books. He was also a *doer* who watched his teacher, obeyed him, and learned from actual practice. Often the disciple lived with his teacher and shared his daily experiences. It was not enough merely to learn academic theory; he had to be able to put the theory into acceptable practice.

I recall the time we established a discipleship program in a church I was pastoring. Our leader carefully selected about fifteen men to meet with him once a week. At the first meeting he explained the course, handed out the materials, and gave them their first assignment. A few of the men were shocked to discover that they would have to do something more than read their Bibles and fill in blanks in a book! The course involved memorizing Scripture, making visits in homes, witnessing to the lost, and sharing the ministry of the church with the people of the city. Well, that was too much for them, so they quietly dropped out. But those men who stayed with it began to grow spiritually and develop effective personal ministries.

In the verses we are studying, our Lord outlined the stages in the experience of his disciples.

1. *They belonged to the Father.*

"Thine they were, and Thou gavest them to Me" (v. 6). We have already considered the profound truth that each believer is the Father's "love gift" to the Son. Now we must consider what our Lord meant when he said, "Thine they were." In what sense did the first disciples belong to the Father?

It seems obvious that they belonged to the Father first of all by *creation.* Paul reminded the Greek philosophers that it is in God that "we live and move and exist" (Acts 17:28).

Job uttered the same truth: "In whose hand is the life of every living thing, and the breath of all mankind?" (Job 12:10). The answer, of course, is God. It was this same truth that Daniel used to warn wicked King Belshazzar that he had better repent: "But the God in whose hand are your life-breath and your ways, you have not glorified" (Dan. 5:23).

We need God because we are the creatures and he is the Creator. When man refused to acknowledge his creature dependence on God, he began to magnify himself as God. If you want to study the sad record of man's devolution, read Romans 1:18–32. Mankind today worships and serves the creature, not the Creator, which explains why the world is in such a mess. Man is playing God, and he is not able to do the job.

The disciples belonged to the Father not only through creation, but also through their belonging to the Jewish nation. They were the sons of the covenant. They were born into that one nation on the face of the earth that God had chosen for himself. Peter's testimony on the housetop in Joppa makes it clear that he was still keeping a "kosher home": "By no means, Lord, for I have never eaten anything unholy [common] and unclean" (Acts 10:14). Until the new Roman policy separated the church from Israel, the early Jewish believers frequented the temple and even shared in some of the traditional Jewish feasts.

They belonged to the Father in a third way: they were a part of that eternal covenant that the Father made with the Son "before the world was." Unknown to these Jewish men, the Father had chosen them in Christ before the foundation of the world (Eph. 1:4), and they would be a part of his "love gift" to the Savior. Unknown to them, the Son would covenant to die for their sins on the cross. God would bypass "the wise and intelligent" and reveal his grace to "babes" (Matt. 11:25). The proud Pharisees with their proper religious system would never stoop low enough to see themselves as sinners. As a result, they would be condemned.

"Thine they were" is a phrase that deals with the preparation of these men for discipleship. The Father arranged for their birth and growth, for their personal development. Psalm 139:13–16 teaches us that the Father is in charge of a baby's conception and growth in the womb. As startling as it may seem, this passage also teaches that the "days that were ordained" for us are already written in God's book! Fatalism? Of course not! Determinism? Wrong again. This is simply the perfect plan of the loving Father who always knows what is best for us. Our genetic inheritance is not human accident; it is divine appointment. Even though we may find ourselves handicapped in some way, we can give what we are to God and know that he will use us for his glory in fulfilling his divine plan.

2. *The Father gave the Word to the Son.*

"For I did not speak on My own initiative," said Jesus, "but the Father Himself who sent Me has given Me commandment, what to say, and what to speak" (John 12:49). He told the Jews, "My teaching is not Mine, but His who sent Me" (John 7:16). Our Lord would talk with his Father and listen for the Father's words. "And the things which I heard from Him [the Father], these I speak to the world" (John 8:26). "I speak these things as the Father taught Me" (John 8:28). "I speak the things which I have seen with My Father" (John 8:38).

Statements like these help us to understand in but a small measure the intimate fellowship that existed between the Father and the Son when Jesus was ministering on earth. It explains why our Lord arose early in the morning for prayer, and why he sometimes withdrew from the crowds. The prophet Isaiah gave a beautiful picture of this fellowship in one of his messianic prophecies. "The Lord GOD has given Me the tongue of disciples, that I may know how to sustain the weary one with a word. He awakens Me morning by morning, He awakens My ear to listen as a disciple. The Lord GOD has opened My ear; and I was not disobedient, nor did I turn back" (Isa. 50:4–5).

The Father gave the words to the Son, just the words that the disciples (and the other people) needed to hear. What did the Son do with these words?

3. *The Son gave the words to the disciples.*

"For the words which Thou gavest Me I have given to them" (v. 8). It was through these words that the Son revealed the Father to them. "I manifested Thy name to the men whom Thou gavest Me out of the world" (v. 6). By "name" is meant God's nature, God's character. It is the Word of God that reveals the Person of God to us. While God does reveal himself in nature and in the workings of divine providence in the world, he is more fully and clearly revealed in the Word which he has given us through his Son.

At this point, we should ask ourselves, "What does John 17 teach about the Word of God?" For one thing, it teaches that the Word of God is *divine in its origin.* When Jesus spoke on earth, it was the Word given to him from heaven. When holy men of God wrote the Word, they were inspired by the Holy Spirit of God (2 Tim. 3:13–17; 2 Peter 1:20–21). The Old Testament prophets said, "Thus saith the Lord!"

When he was ministering on earth, our Lord set his seal of approval on the Bible. He quoted from the Old Testament Scriptures in such a way that he affirmed their truth and authority. He promised that the Holy Spirit would assist in the writing of the Gospels (John 14:26). That same Holy Spirit would guide believers into truth, which suggests the writing of the Epistles; and the Spirit would also reveal "things to come," which points to the Book of Revelation (John 16:13).

The fact that Jesus called the Word of God "truth" is evidence of its divine origin. The Bible is not just true; it is *truth*, which is the essence of that which is true. This would indicate that we can trust the Word of God in whatever it declares. "Therefore I esteem right all Thy precepts concerning everything, I hate every false way" (Ps. 119:128). God's Word is not only inspired, it is inerrant.

This Word is *a gift from God*. This is stated in verses 8 and 14. The Word is not man's record of his attempt to find God; it is God's record to man of all that God had done to seek and save the lost. The Word is a gift to us because God paid the price for us to have it. Never underestimate the cost of the Word of God. God paid a price, and the men whom the Spirit used also paid a price. When we cease to appreciate the Word of God as a precious gift, we will also cease to appreciate the Word of God as the nourishment of our souls and the guide for our lives.

The Word *generates faith*. "They believed that Thou didst send Me" (v. 8). "So faith comes from hearing, and hearing by the word of Christ" (Rom. 10:17). "I used to think I should close my Bible and pray for faith," said evangelist D. L. Moody, "but I came to see that it was in studying the Word that I was to get faith."

God's Word is called "the word of faith" (Rom. 10:8). It not only demands faith on our part, but it creates faith by its inherent power. "For no word of God shall be void of power" (Luke 1:37 ASV). This truth is often illustrated in the miracles that Jesus performed. The man with the withered hand was commanded to stretch out that hand, something he could not do; *yet he did it*. The palsied man who could not walk was commanded to walk, *and he did it*. God's commandments are also God's enablements. "For the word of God is living and active. . . ." (Heb. 4:12).

The Word also *reveals Christ to us*. "Now they have come to know that everything Thou hast given Me is from Thee"

(v. 7). "They believed that Thou didst send Me" (v. 8). It is the Word of God that reveals the Son of God. Jesus said, "It is these [Scriptures] that bear witness of Me" (John 5:39). "And beginning with Moses and with all the prophets, He explained to them the things concerning Himself in all the Scriptures" (Luke 24:27).

The Scriptures reveal the person of Jesus Christ, that he is the Savior sent by the Father; and they reveal the riches of Christ, all that the Father has given to the Son to share with us. "The Father had given all things into His [Christ's] hands. . . ." (John 13:3). It is our privilege to read and study the Word and to discover how rich we are in Jesus Christ.

Finally, it is the Word that *gives us assurance.* The disciples *knew* that Jesus was the Son of God. They *understood* that he had come from God to the world. This was their own testimony: "Now we know that You know all things . . . by this we believe that You came from God" (John 16:30). I have often counseled with people who lacked assurance of their salvation. In most instances, I have urged these troubled people to read the Word of God, especially John's Gospel and the first Epistle of John. In most cases, the doubts and fears disappeared as the assurance of the Word got ahold of their minds and hearts. Like the Samaritans in Sychar, they had a firsthand experience with Christ through his Word. "It is no longer because of what you said that we believe," they told the woman who witnessed to them, "for we have heard for ourselves and know that this One is indeed the Savior of the world" (John 4:42).

We have seen three of the stages in the disciples' spiritual experience: they belonged to the Father; the Father gave the Word to the Son; and the Son gave the Word to the disciples.

4. *The disciples received the Word and believed.*

The Word of God is like seed, and it must be received into the "soil" of the heart if it is to take root and produce

63

fruit (Luke 8:4–15). God prepares the heart for the Word (Acts 16:14–15), but we can harden our hearts against God's Word (Heb. 3:7–19). "Take care how you listen," Jesus warned his disciples (Luke 8:18). The way we treat the Bible is the way we treat Jesus Christ, for he is the living Word (John 1:1, 14) and the Bible is the written Word. If a father paid no attention to his son's words, he would be admitting that his son was not important to him. If we ignore or neglect God's Word, or if we treat it carelessly, we are admitting to God that he is not important in our lives.

"And for this reason we also constantly thank God that when you received from us the word of God's message, you accepted it not as the word of men, but for what it really is, the word of God, which also performs its work in you who believe" (1 Thess. 2:13). The disciples made mistakes, to be sure, and they often did not grasp what Jesus was saying; but in spite of their failings they respected and received the Word of God which he taught. Often the meaning and dynamic of that Word did not come to them until later, but none of that Word was wasted (see John 2:17, 22; and 12:16). This Word is not wasted because the Holy Spirit of God can remind us of it when we need it (John 14:26).

When I was a child in Sunday school, and then a teenager in confirmation class, I did not always understand the Scriptures that we studied and sometimes had to memorize. But the seed was planted in my heart. When I became a Christian at the age of sixteen, the Spirit of God began to teach me the truths contained in those Scriptures. None of that Word was wasted. In my ministry today, I am amazed at what the Spirit brings to my mind as I preach, write, and witness. He is able to bring out of the treasury of our hearts "things new and old" (Matt. 13:52).

Effective discipleship depends on close attention to the Word of God. The Spirit of God teaches us from the Word, and then he directs our lives into circumstances that force us to trust the Word and act upon it. It has well been said that life is a school in which you learn what the lessons were *after* you take the test. Jesus taught his disciples and then sent them out to serve. They would come back, report on their ministry, and then learn again the lessons they had forgotten. It was only after they had proved what they had learned that Jesus would impart new truths to them.

Just as Jesus shared the Word with his disciples when he was on earth, so he shares it with us by his Spirit (John 16:12–15). The Spirit does not give new revelations, for the divine revelation is settled once and for all in the Scriptures. But he does give divine *illumination* as he shows us new truths and new application of old truths. The Christian who studies his Bible is not searching *for* truth, but searching *into* truth.

5. *The disciples kept the Word.*

"They have kept Thy word" (v. 6). The word "kept" means "obeyed." They received the Word, believed it, and acted upon it. It is not enough to appreciate the Word and hold it in high esteem; we must also apply it. "Never think that Jesus commanded a trifle," said D. L. Moody, "nor dare to trifle with anything He has commanded." A true disciple is much more than a learner; he is one who lives what he learns. It is not in the studying of the Bible that we grow spiritually, but in the doing of what God has taught us. "But prove yourselves doers of the word, and not merely hearers who delude themselves" (James 1:22).

But the word "kept" also carries the idea of "guarded." The disciples guarded the Word. It was a valuable treasure to them. "The law of Thy mouth is better to me than thousands of gold and silver pieces" (Ps. 119:72). "Therefore I love Thy commandments above gold, yes, above fine gold" (Ps. 119:127). "I rejoice at Thy word, as one who finds great spoil" (Ps. 119:162).

I sometimes get the impression that some zealous Christians today are so concerned about *guarding* the Word that they forget to *obey* it. They think they are serving God by their "holy crusades" of accusation and attack, crusades that are not always based on truth or motivated by love. I recall with a sad heart a young man who used to stand at the steps of our church building and pass out literature that condemned certain schools and preachers. I asked him why he didn't pass out gospel tracts to lost sinners. When we asked him to go away from the church building, or else to come in to worship, he shouted: "I'm a fighting fundamentalist and I don't care who knows it! You people are not preaching the truth!" I appreciate any believer who wants to *defend* the faith, but his belligerent attitude made a *mockery* of the faith. The best way to defend the Bible is to practice it.

The disciples kept the Word because they loved Jesus Christ. Jesus said, "If anyone loves Me, he will keep my word; and My Father will love him, and We will come to him, and make Our abode with him. He who does not love Me does not keep My words. . . ." (John 14:23–24). Obedience and faithfulness that are motivated by love will glorify God and build up his church. There is a deep and satisfying communion among the obedient Christian and the Father and the Savior. "The one who says, 'I have come to know Him,' and does not keep His commandments, is a liar, and the truth is not in him; but whoever keeps His word, in him the love of God has truly been perfected. . . ." (1 John 2:4–5).

Obedience that is not motivated by love cannot produce the spiritual fruit that God wants from his children. If we obey because of fear (God may punish me!) or because of greed (If I obey, God must bless me!), then we cannot expect that close communion with the Father that Jesus promised to those who keep the Word. "If you love Me, you will keep My commandments" (John 14:15).

6. *They shared the Word with others.*

The Lord Jesus sent them into the world (John 17:18) that they might win others through their witness of the Word (John 17:20). There is a church in the world today because believers have been faithful to share the Word down through the centuries. "And the things which you have heard from me in the presence of many witnesses, these entrust to faithful men, who will be able to teach others also" (2 Tim. 2:2). We will have more to say about this exciting ministry of witnessing when we get to the study of that section of the prayer.

Suffice it to say now that a true disciple is not a reservoir but a gushing fountain, an artesian well of spiritual blessing. He does not live to get; he lives to give. What he receives from the Lord, he shares with others; and in sharing, he receives even more. He is careful to guard the precious spiritual investment God has put into his life, but he also invests that treasure in the lives of others. Money put into the bank is both protected and invested, and it helps to produce more wealth. The spiritual truth of the Word that we share with others helps to produce "spiritual dividends" that will last eternally.

Each of us needs to examine his or her own heart to see if what we profess is true discipleship. Do we receive the Word daily from the Lord? Do we guard it and obey it because we love him? Do we share it with others? Do we have faith and assurance because of the Word and Word only?

"If you abide in My word," said Jesus, "then you are truly disciples of Mine; and you shall know the truth, and the truth shall make you free" (John 8:31–32).

SAVED AND SAFE

I ask on their behalf; I do not ask on behalf of the world, but of those whom Thou hast given Me; for they are Thine; and all things that are Mine are Thine, and Thine are Mine; and I have been glorified in them. And I am no more in the world; and yet they themselves are in the world, and I come to Thee. Holy Father, keep them in Thy name, the name which Thou hast given Me, that they may be one, even as We are. While I was with them, I was keeping them in Thy name which Thou hast given Me; and I guarded them, and not one of them perished but the son of perdition, that the Scripture might be fulfilled.
—John 17:9–12

e are living in enemy territory, so beware! The world system hates Christ while pretending to honor God. Satan prowls about as a roaring lion. The very atmosphere that we breathe is poisoned with "the lust of the flesh and the lust of the eyes

69

and the boastful pride of life" (1 John 2:16). The world system around us appeals to the flesh within us so that we fight a steady battle against temptation. How, then, can the dedicated believer remain safe and secure in such a dangerous world?

Our security is in Jesus Christ. When you have trusted him as your Savior, you have a spiritual security that nothing can destroy. I know, it seems too good to be true; but even salvation itself is too good to be true! Our personal relationship to the Father through Jesus Christ is unchanged and unchangeable, even though our *fellowship* with him may change from day to day. Our *union* with Christ is secure, no matter what may alter our *communion*. Let's consider several truths presented in verses 9–12, as well as in the previous verses, that indicate and affirm that the believer is secure in Christ.

1. *Christ prayed for us.*

"I ask on their behalf . . . Holy Father, keep them in Thy name. . . ." (vv. 9 and 11).

To be sure, he was praying for his disciples; but our spiritual oneness in Christ makes up a part of that fellowship. Furthermore, we today stand in a similar relationship to the Savior as the disciples did in that day. It is unthinkable that our Lord would pray for that small body of believers and ignore the needs of the whole church.

The Father always answered the prayers of the Son. At the tomb of his friend Lazarus, Jesus said: "Father, I thank Thee that Thou heardest Me. And I knew that Thou hearest Me always. . . ." (John 11:41–42). The Son would surely never ask anything outside the Father's will, and the Father would never refuse the requests of the "Son of His love" (Col. 1:13 [margin]). If our Lord asked the Father to protect and guard the believers, that request would be granted.

The word "keep" means "to watch over, to care for, to preserve." It is used in Acts 16:23 to describe the jailer's guarding of Paul and Silas. In verse 12, Jesus also used the word "guarded," which is a different Greek word meaning "taking custody, giving protection." The *keeping* is the result of the *guarding*. Both words affirm safety and security.

2. *Christ is now praying for us in heaven.*

"And I am no more in the world" (v. 11). In this prayer, our Lord looked upon the work of redemption as something already finished. He was to leave the world and return to the Father in heaven, and there he would enter into his "unfinished work" of interceding for his church.

We must not imagine our Lord's heavenly intercession as the constant repeating of prayers before the Father. Nor should we imagine that the Father is against us and the Son must placate him! Both the Father and the Son love us and are concerned for our welfare and spiritual success. The very presence of Jesus Christ at the throne of heaven is his intercession for us. He represents us. We pray to the Father through the authority of the name of the Son. We come to the High Priest at the throne of grace, and he gives us "grace to help in time of need" (Heb. 4:16). This keeps us from sinning. But if we do sin, then we come to our advocate and confess our sins and find forgiveness (1 John 1:9–2:2).

This intercessory work of Jesus is an assurance to us of our security in the family of God. "Who is the one who condemns? Christ Jesus is He who died, yes, rather who was raised, who is at the right hand of God, who also intercedes for us" (Rom. 8:34). There are many who would condemn us for our sins and failures; in fact, we often condemn ourselves. But, the one who has the right to condemn will not do it. "There is therefore now no condemnation for those who are in Christ Jesus" (Rom. 8:1).

The Old Testament high priest had two sets of precious stones on his beautiful garments. He had twelve stones on the breastplate over his heart and six stones on each of his shoulders. These stones represented the twelve tribes of

Israel. The picture is most encouraging: our Lord carries his own over his heart and on his shoulders. He bears us in love. He intercedes for us because he loves us and wants the very best for us. When he was on earth, our Lord went through all of the circumstances of life—the testings and temptations—that he might be able to sympathize with us in our trials. The High Priest who prays for us loves us and understands just how we feel.

In the Old Testament economy, the high priests died and others had to take their place. But Jesus Christ can never die. "But He [Jesus] . . . because He abides forever, holds His priesthood permanently. Hence, also, He is able to save forever those who draw near to God through Him, since He always lives to make intercession for them" (Heb. 7:24–25). Note the logic of the writer: because Jesus Christ lives forever, he has a permanent priesthood, and this permanent priesthood means *salvation forever.*

And, I might add, if the Father always answered the Son's prayers when the Son was in his humiliation on earth, will the Father not answer them now that the Son is glorified in heaven? Furthermore, if the Son, during his days of humble earthly ministry, was able to guard his own and keep them, certainly he would be able to continue this success now that he is enthroned in heaven. It seems reasonable, doesn't it?

This means that believers today are just as safe and secure as were the twelve apostles when Jesus was with them on earth. Peter was attacked by Satan, tempted, and denied the Lord; but the Lord protected him and brought him to fellowship again. Peter's faith wavered and he began to sink into the waters, but Jesus guarded him and rescued him. Thomas had his doubts, but Jesus lovingly encouraged him and led him into glorious assurance. Philip was worried about finding enough money to buy food to feed over five thousand people, but Jesus had the problem all solved. On more than one occasion, the Lord kept his disciples out of difficulties, but even when they found themselves in trouble he was there to assist them.

3. *We are the Father's gift to the Son.* Christ is not praying for the lost world. He is praying for "those whom Thou [the Father] hast given Me" (v. 9). The church prays for the lost (Matt. 5:44; 1 Tim. 2:1), but the Savior prays for the church. Believers are the Father's special "love gift" to the Son, and it is unthinkable that the Father would permit this gift of love to fail by one believer being lost. (We will consider the special case of Judas in the next chapter.) Salvation is wholly of God's grace (Eph. 2:8–9). If we could not be saved by our good works, why should we be condemned *after we are saved* because of some sin or act of disobedience? If God, who knows all things, knew that we would fail, why would he have given us his Son in the first place? Either we are saved by grace and grace alone, or we are not saved at all. "But if it is by grace, it is no longer on the basis of works, otherwise grace is no longer grace" (Rom. 11:6).

I cannot emphasize too strongly the fact that our salvation is part of a vast eternal plan, conceived in the heart and mind of God "before the world was." God does not start something he cannot finish. "For I am confident of this very thing, that He who began a good work in you will perfect it until the day of Christ Jesus" (Phil. 1:6). "For we are His workmanship, created in Christ Jesus for good works, which God prepared beforehand, that we should walk in them" (Eph. 2:10).

Not only are we the Father's love gift to the Son, but eternal life is the Son's love gift to all who believe on him. Eternal life is a gift (John 17:2). We do not earn it; we cannot merit it. It is a gift. Would God, who knows all things, give us such a costly gift if he knew we would fail? Can our sins alter the faithfulness of God? "For the gifts and the calling of God are irrevocable" (Rom. 11:29).

Salvation must be wholly by God's grace if God is to get the glory. This leads us to another spiritual truth.

4. *God is glorified in believers.*

"I have been glorified in them," said Jesus (v. 10). Not one word about the failings of the disciples! There is no mention of Peter's impetuous speeches, or James and John wanting to burn up a Samaritan village, or the disciples' boasting that they would remain true to the Master. What a reassuring statement to all of us! When Jesus Christ presents his church to the Father in glory, he will say, "I have been glorified in them." But if any believer should "lose his salvation," God would lose his glory. The very glory of God is at stake in our safety and security.

This explains why Jesus prayed, "Holy Father, keep them in Thy name. . . ." (v. 11). The Father's name is mentioned four times in this prayer. Jesus manifested the Father's name to his disciples (v. 6). He prayed that they might be kept in that name (v. 11). Jesus had kept them in that name (v. 12). Jesus had declared that name to be his own (v. 26). By "the name," of course, is meant the Father's character. *The security of the believer is related intimately to the very character of God.*

The ultimate purpose of our salvation is the glory of God. Three times in Ephesians 1 we are told that we are saved for the praise of God's glory (vv. 6, 12, 14); "so that in all things God may be glorified through Jesus Christ, to whom belongs the glory and dominion forever and ever" (1 Peter 4:11). Sixteen times in John 13–17 our Lord talked about glory. He had glorified the Father on the earth (John 17:4), and now his disciples and his church would take his place to glorify the Father on the earth (v. 18).

If a true believer ever "lost his salvation," God would lose far more than would that believer. The believer does not deserve salvation, so he would have "lost" something that was not inherently his to begin with. But God would lose glory, and God deserves to be glorified because he is God. It would bring disgrace to the name and character of God if one of his children did not go to heaven.

While on the subject of glory, we should note that Christ has *already given us his glory.* "And the glory which Thou hast given Me I have given to them" (v. 22). The tense of the verb indicates an act completed in the past with the results carrying into the present and future. The same tense is used of the Father's giving the glory to the Son as with the Son's giving glory to the believers. The Father will not take the glory from the Son, and the Son will not take the glory from the church. The matter is settled once and for all. This explains why Paul could write in Romans 8:30: "and whom He justified, these He also glorified." Not "will glorify when they arrive in heaven," but *glorified.* It is done!

When you consider the majesty of God's character, the glory of his eternal attributes, you cannot help but acknowledge that he can and does keep his own. Certainly he has the power to do it. He is too wise to make a mistake. He is faithful to himself and to his Word even if we are unfaithful. "If we are faithless, He remains faithful; for He cannot deny Himself" (2 Tim. 2:13).

Someone asked the great financier J. P. Morgan, "What is the best collateral a person can give for a loan?" and Morgan replied, "Character." God's character is the best collateral we can have that our eternal salvation is secure in Christ.

5. *God's church is one in unity.*

"Holy Father, keep them in Thy name . . . that they may be one, even as We are" (v. 11).

The emphasis today is on *individual* salvation. "Each one reach one" is a popular motto in our churches. Of course, sinners are saved individually. Our Lord, when he was ministering on earth, took time to talk to people personally and individually—Nicodemus, the Samaritan woman, Zacchaeus, and many others come to mind. But even though faith in Christ is personal and individual, union with Christ involves all believers. That individual believer becomes a part of the body of Christ, the church, and his life from then on must reflect this great fact.

The spiritual unity of believers is an important theme in this prayer. Jesus mentions it not only in verse 11, but also in verses 21–23. There are several illustrations of this great truth given in Scripture: the vine and the branches (John 15:1–10), the body and the members (1 Cor. 12), the stones in the temple (1 Peter 2:4–10). Because we are related to Christ, we are related to each other. We belong to each other and we need each other. I often say to the newlyweds after the marriage ceremony, "Now, remember, it's no longer *yours* and *mine*, but *ours*."

There is an epidemic of "individualism" in the Christian world today. We seem to be living in the Book of Judges: every man is doing what is right in his own eyes (Judg. 17:6; 18:1; 19:1; and 21:25). We recite the Lord's Prayer and fail to notice that the first word is "Our." It is not "My Father" but "Our Father." We belong to each other *even when we pray*. In more than forty years of ministry, I have seen the individualistic spirit divide God's people, split churches, transform friends into enemies, and hinder the progress of the gospel. If a preacher does not get his own way, he takes his friends from the church, goes up the street, and starts a new church. If a church member disagrees with his pastor, he takes his family and either meets in a home or starts attending another church, where (more than likely) he will soon have another disagreement.

We will study this important subject of spiritual unity in a later chapter. In our present context, the truth of the unity of the believer with God and with other believers relates directly to the matter of security. We are united to Christ by his Spirit (1 Cor. 12:13) and we are united to one another. If a true Christian could fall away and "lose his salvation," then this spiritual union is not dependable and the church can never be completed. We cannot fully relate to one another unless we are sure of our relationship to God. This modern emphasis only on *personal* salvation makes us lose sight of the grandeur and glory of God's church. I am not minimizing our personal experience with Christ, but I am affirming that it is not the primary goal that God has in mind. He is building his church. He is building up the body of Christ. The glory and greatness of our personal salvation is but a reflection of what God is doing *corporately* in and through his church. I realize that this "corporate body" never meets, that it is a concept in the mind of God that will have fruition in eternity. But this does not mean his church is not real or important. What we do in our local fellowships should be governed by what God wants to do in his church, the corporate body.

The greatness of the church encourages me to believe that salvation is secure in Christ. Not one member of the Body will be lost; not one stone in the temple will lose its place; not one branch on the vine will fail to bear fruit to one degree or another.

 6. *Christ finished his work.*

The reason our Lord could return to heaven was that his work on earth was finished. "I glorified Thee on the earth, having accomplished the work which Thou hast given Me to do" (v. 4). In a previous study we learned of the greatness of this work. How does our Lord's finished work relate to the subject of the security of the believer?

When Christ died, he died for all of our sins. Some people have the idea that Jesus died only for their *past* sins, so if they sin again they lose their salvation and must be saved again. (Of course, logically this would mean that Jesus would have to die again for sins he didn't die for the first time, and that makes the cross something ridiculous.) *Our sins were not in the past when Jesus died; they were all future.* But even if we had been alive at the time of his death, it would have made no difference. The work of Christ on the cross was an eternal work, planned from before the foundation of the world, and time cannot affect it. He died for all the sins of all the people of all the world. He stretched out his arms on the cross and reached back to Adam and forward to the end of human history. He bore the whole burden of sin once and for all.

This means that when the sinner trusts Christ *all* of his sins are forgiven—past, present, and future. "He made you alive together with Him, having forgiven us all our transgressions" (Col. 2:13). Remember, Jesus Christ did not die to make salvation available. *He died to save us.* Now, either he finished the work or he did not. If he did not, then we are still in our sins. *But he finished the work of redemption.* He did not "make the down payment" and ask us to keep up the installments. He paid the full price himself.

Our security in Christ is not an excuse for careless living. It is a basis for communion with God, unity with God's people, and ministry to a lost world. Each of these themes will be discussed in chapters that follow.

Our response to this great truth ought to be one of gratitude, worship, and adoration.

"Worthy is the Lamb that was slain to receive power and riches and wisdom and might and honor and glory and blessing" (Rev. 5:12).

7

The Man Who Should Never Have Been Born

> While I was with them, I was keeping them in Thy name which Thou hast given Me; and I guarded them, and not one of them perished but the son of perdition, that the Scripture might be fulfilled.
>
> —John 17:12

There are some names that have made their way into the dictionary: Jezebel, Benedict Arnold, Quisling (he betrayed Norway to the Nazis), Casanova, Don Juan, and Brutus.

And Judas Iscariot.

To call someone "Judas" would be to classify him with the most infamous traitor in human history. "For the Son of Man is to go, just as it is written of Him," said Jesus, "but woe to that man by whom the Son of Man is betrayed! It would have been good for that man if he had not been born" (Mark 14:21).

In all of the lists of the names of the twelve disciples, Peter is always listed first and Judas Iscariot last. The New Testament tells us more about these two men than all the other ten disciples combined. Judas was a popular name, as was Simon. There are nine Simons found in the New Testament and six Judases. (Simon and Judas Maccabaeus, brothers, were popular Jewish heroes during the period between the Testaments.) Today nobody in the Christian world would call a son Judas, even though the name means "praise" and is great in Old Testament history. The dictionary tells me that a "Judas kiss" is a false expression of affection and that a "Judas hole" is a hidden slit in the wall through which guards spy on prisoners. Nobody wants the name "Judas" attached to himself.

Let's consider the different acts in the drama of the tragedy of Judas Iscariot.

1. *The disciple*

After a night of prayer, our Lord came down from the mountain and chose twelve men to become his disciples (Luke 6:12–16). Judas Iscariot was among them. If, as many scholars believe, the name "Iscariot" comes from "man of Kerioth," then Judas was probably the only disciple who was not a Galilean, for the city of Kerioth belonged to the tribe of Judah (Josh. 15:25).

Did Jesus know what Judas was like and what he would do? The indications are that he did. "For Jesus knew from the beginning who they were who did not believe, and who it was that would betray Him" (John 6:64). "For He knew all men, and . . . He did not need anyone to bear witness concerning man for He Himself knew what was in man" (John 2:24–25). If Jesus knew from the beginning that Simon would become a rock, he certainly knew that Judas would become a traitor.

Then why did he call him to be a disciple? Because it was the will of God. Our Lord prayed all night before he called these men. I wonder if a part of that praying was not devoted to asking the Father for special help to deal with Judas.

Over the centuries, Bible students and philosophers have wrestled with the mystery of Judas, and several "solutions" have been offered. One is that Judas was a *victim*. Somebody had to betray Jesus, and Judas was elected to do it. After all, there were prophecies to be fulfilled! But this approach to the problem makes Judas a mere robot, a pawn in God's omnipotent hand. It robs Judas of humanity and of responsibility, yet the Bible makes it clear that Judas was held responsible for what he did. In fact, Judas himself admitted his personal guilt: "I have sinned by betraying innocent blood" (Matt. 27:4). Nobody, including God, forced Judas to betray the Son of God.

Another approach to the "victim" theory is that Judas was Satan's victim, not God's. It argues that God turned Judas over to the devil so that the Old Testament Scriptures could be fulfilled. But this theory makes a devil out of God! "Let no one say when he is tempted, 'I am being tempted by God'; for God cannot be tempted by evil, and He Himself does not tempt anyone" (James 1:13). That Satan was involved in Judas Iscariot's sin, no one can deny. Satan put the idea of treachery in Judas's heart (John 13:2), and when Judas yielded, "Satan then entered into him" (John 13:27; also see Luke 22:1–4). The idea was there long before Judas entered the upper room, for he had already contacted the Jewish leaders. Jesus certainly knew that Satan was after Judas, for he said, "One of you is a devil" (John 6:70). The description fits, for Judas, like Satan, was a liar and a murderer (John 8:44).

If Judas was not a victim, is it possible he was a *hero?* Several noble attempts have been made to rescue Judas from disgrace, but none of them has really succeeded. Thomas DeQuincey, the British author, wrote an essay along these lines, claiming that Judas was really a courageous man who only wanted to force Jesus to declare himself "King of the Jews" and thus rescue the nation from Roman dictatorship. His motives were good, but perhaps the method Judas used was not good. The whole scheme backfired and Jesus was crucified. Humiliated, Judas committed suicide. This is a clever theory, but it has nothing in Scripture to support it. To begin with, Jesus had made it very clear to the disciples that he did not intend to establish a political kingdom. Judas would have known this. Furthermore, our Lord did not need anybody's "prompting" to accomplish God's will. He was not a vacillating young prophet. He knew what he was doing and when the Father wanted him to act.

There are two variations on this theme. One is that Judas, a loyal Jew, knew that Jesus was a false prophet, so he betrayed him for the sake of his nation. However, if Judas had that kind of proof available, the Sanhedrin would not have needed to hire false witnesses to testify against Christ. The second variation is that Judas saw trouble coming and really wanted to restrain Jesus only for the sake of protecting the nation. After the Passover, Jesus would be free to minister again, but the situation would no longer be hazardous. Obviously, this is woolly thinking. The disciples knew that the Jewish rulers were out to kill Jesus (John 8:59; 10:31; 11:8). Once they got their hands on him, they would do more than restrain him!

The problem that comes to the Christian believer is not that Judas was a victim or a hero, but that he was possibly an *apostate*. Was Judas a true believer who "fell from the faith" and lost his salvation? It is my sincere conviction that Judas was never saved at all. In spite of the fact that he was baptized by John the Baptist (Acts 1:21–22), ordained an apostle by Jesus (Luke 6:12–16), and companied with the other disciples, Judas was not a true believer at all.

Jesus made it clear that *Judas never believed on him.* "'But there are some of you who do not believe.' For Jesus knew from the beginning who they were who did not believe, and who it was that would betray Him" (John 6:64). Judas is classified with those who did not believe. It was in that same context that Jesus called Judas "a devil" (John 6:70). Not "a demon," or even "a demonized man," but "a devil."

Jesus also made it clear that *Judas had never been cleansed.* "For He knew the one who was betraying Him; for this reason He said, 'Not all of you are clean'" (John 13:11). Now, if Judas had never been cleansed, that means he had never been saved; for salvation means being washed clean from our sins (Rev. 1:5).

Jesus declared that *Judas had never been chosen in electing grace.* "I do not speak of all of you. I know the ones I have chosen; but it is that the Scripture may be fulfilled, 'He who eats My bread has lifted up his heel against Me'" (John 13:18). The King James Version of John 17:12 gives the impression that Judas was one of those whom the Father had given to the Son; but the New American Standard Bible and the New International Version give us a different picture. The New International Version says: "While I was with them, I protected them and kept them safe by that name you gave me." In both translations, the "given" phrase is connected with the name and not with the disciples. The fact that Judas was chosen to be a disciple (John 6:70–71) was not proof that he was one of those given by the Father to the Son.

Additional proof of this fact is found in John 18:1–9. When our Lord was arrested in the Garden, he protected the eleven disciples who stood with him. "Let these go their way," he requested of the soldiers. John adds: "that the word might be fulfilled which He spoke, 'Of those whom Thou hast given Me I lost not one'" (John 18:8–9). It is obvious that Jesus was not speaking about Judas, for Judas was not standing with the other disciples. There was no need for Jesus to protect Judas because Judas was already on the side of the enemy. If Judas had been one of God's chosen, these words of Jesus make no sense.

Judas was not a victim, a hero, or an apostate. He was a lost sinner who never trusted Jesus Christ and who went to eternal condemnation (Acts 1:25) because he did not take advantage of the tremendous opportunities he had. Why he acted as he did is not fully known, although I will make some suggestions later in this chapter.

2. *The thief*

Judas was the treasurer of the disciple band (John 12:1–8). One of his jobs was to distribute money to the poor (John 12:5 and 13:26–30). John makes it clear that Judas had been pilfering money out of the treasury: "he was a thief, and as he had the money box, he used to pilfer what was put into it" (John 12:6). None of the disciples knew what Judas was doing, but Jesus knew. In fact, I wonder if our Lord's many warnings about covetousness and wealth were not aimed at Judas. No wonder Judas criticized Mary for her extravagance in spending a year's wages on ointment so that she might anoint Jesus. Just think of what a year's wages would have done for the treasury—and Judas!

Never underestimate the power of covetousness. The desire to be rich is fraught with all kinds of dangers. "But those who want to get rich fall into temptation and a snare and many foolish and harmful desires which plunge men into ruin and destruction. For the love of money is a root of all sorts of evil. . . ." (1 Tim. 6:9–10). The word "destruction" is the same as "perdition" in John 17:12.

Covetousness will lead a person to commit all kinds of sins in order to get what he wants. "Thou shalt not covet" is the last of the Ten Commandments, but covetousness can lead to the breaking of the other nine. If a person is covetous, he makes money his god. Covetousness will make a person lie, steal, even murder, to get what he lusts after. Judas permitted covetousness to take over in his life, and it led to his ruin. His life was not directed by "What is right?" but by "What will you give me?" (Matt. 26:14–15).

It is worth noting that Judas's question "Why this waste?" (Matt. 26:8) contains the same word that is translated "destruction" and "perdition." Judas was concerned about Mary's wasting the ointment, while he himself was headed for waste! (As though *anything* lovingly given to Jesus is ever wasted!) He would be known as "the son of perdition—the son of waste." It shocks us that Judas could sell the Lord Jesus for thirty pieces of silver, the price of a slave. Covetousness blinds a person to the true value of life and enslaves him to the insatiable appetite for more and more money and things.

What did Judas do with the money that he pilfered? It has been suggested by some students of the Bible that Judas bought himself a piece of property. The thirty pieces of silver, of course, were used to buy the "potter's field" for the burial of strangers (Matt. 27:1–10). But Acts 1:18 states that Judas "acquired a field with the price of his wickedness. . . ." The word "acquired" is literally "procured for one's self, purchased." It is a different word from that used in Matthew 27:7 describing the priests' purchase of the potter's field. In fact, two different words are used for "field."

The suggestion is that two different purchases and two different fields are involved. The priests used the thirty pieces of silver to purchase the potter's field for a cemetery. Judas used the money stolen from the treasury to purchase a little plot of ground for himself. He went to this property after he had given back the money, and there he hanged himself. He could not have hanged himself at the potter's field for he did not know that the priests were even going to purchase such a field. (And it is not likely that they would purchase it immediately, during Passover.) It seems reasonable that he would escape to his own property—land that had cost him his conscience and his soul—and there end his life.

85

Acts 1:18 suggests that his suicide was not quickly discovered and that his body distended and burst. If the rope broke, this would explain why the body fell forward.

The priests called the potter's field "the Field of Blood" (Matt. 27:8) because it was purchased with "blood money." But Judas's field was also called "Field of Blood" (Acts 1:19) because of his blood having been shed there. It is not reasonable that the priests would purchase a field in which a man committed suicide. Such a field would be considered unclean.

Judas the thief secured his field but lost his life. "For what does it profit a man to gain the whole world, and to forfeit his soul?" (Mark 8:36).

3. *The traitor*

The psychology of Judas is a riddle wrapped up in a puzzle and locked in an enigma. That Judas had listened to John the Baptist and submitted to John's baptism of repentance is clear from Acts 1:21–22. Apparently he did nothing while he was a disciple that even hinted at his true spiritual condition, nor did Jesus ever give any hints. If anything, our Lord did all he could to rescue Judas. Certainly many of our Lord's teachings must have pierced Judas's heart. The repeated warnings against love of money should have stopped Judas, but he did not heed them. Our Lord's denunciation of hypocrisy made no impact on the false apostle.

When you read the account of our Lord's upper room ministry, you can see how he tried one last time to get to Judas's heart. True to Jewish custom, Jesus kissed Judas (and the other disciples) when they came to the Passover feast. He even gave Judas the seat of honor, at his left. He washed Judas's feet. He gave Judas the token of friendship, the sop (bread dipped in the bitter herbs). This act should have sealed a bond of friendship, but instead it triggered treachery. Jesus even spoke words of warning that only Judas would fully understand. "You are clean, but not all of you"

(John 13:10–11). His quotation from Psalm 41:9 (John 13:18) was especially meaningful to Judas, who obviously did not tremble at God's Word.

Then Jesus spoke plainly, "Truly I say to you that one of you will betray Me" (Matt. 26:21). Each of the disciples, including Judas, responded with, "Surely not I!" (Matt. 26:25). Jesus clearly warned Judas with his "woe to that man by whom the Son of Man is betrayed!" (Matt. 26:24). But Jesus did not openly name Judas. His giving him the sop was normal, for Judas was at his left. Only John knew the truth; and by then, Judas had arisen from the table and gone out. The disciples thought he was going to give something to the poor. Until the very end, Jesus protected Judas and gave him opportunity to repent.

Why would Judas do such a thing? Nobody knows for sure, but we can conjecture about it and try to find some answers.

One suggestion is that Judas was a loyal Jew with great messianic expectations. He wanted to see God's kingdom established once again in Israel. This is why Judas was so attracted to John the Baptist. But John the Baptist was not a miracle worker, and Jesus was, so it was easy for Judas to change his allegiance and follow Jesus. Early in our Lord's ministry, he attracted great crowds and proclaimed the advent of God's kingdom. But then the emphasis of his ministry changed, so much so that even John the Baptist in prison was wondering if he were the Messiah (Matt. 11:1–6). It seemed clear to Judas that Jesus would not (or could not) fulfill his messianic dreams.

Since he was already publicly identified with Christ and the disciples, Judas could not abandon ship and still maintain any kind of credibility. So he stayed with the movement and tried to get out of it whatever he could. He began to steal money from the treasury. (It must have broken Judas's heart when the rich young ruler decided not to follow Jesus.) Over the months, the cancer of covetousness began to eat at his heart, along with the cancer of bitterness. If Jesus failed, Judas would fail with him. But why fail? If Judas turned state's evidence, he could get money and satisfy his vengeance at the same time. He would be accepted by the religious establishment and could spend the rest of his days enjoying the fruits of his treachery.

As previously noted, Judas was not a Galilean. He came from Kerioth in Judah. The people in Galilee enjoyed more freedom than those in Judah, for Judea was ruled by a Roman governor. It is possible that Judas's nationalistic spirit helped to lead to his downfall. Satan had several footholds in this man's life: his love of money, his growing hatred of Jesus, and his political zeal. Betraying Jesus would give Judas the satisfaction of meeting all three needs at the same time.

Of course, all of this is conjecture. But it makes sense, and it is certainly true to human nature. This we do know, that Judas betrayed the greatest love that had ever been shown on earth.

4. *The suicide*

We have already discussed some aspects of this terrible act, but there are some other factors that should be considered. First of all, Judas did not repent of his sins. "Then when Judas, who had betrayed Him, saw that He had been condemned, he felt remorse. . . ." (Matt. 27:3). Remorse and regret are not the same as repentance. Of course, Judas had yielded himself to the power of Satan and it was now too late.

But why suicide? Why not just flee the country and make the best of it? Because Satan is a murderer (John 8:44) and a destroyer (Rev. 9:11). He comes first as the deceiving serpent ("You can get away with this!") but then turns into the destroying lion (1 Peter 5:8). He uses despair and guilt to drive people to self-destruction. He preys upon the hopeless and the helpless, and he convinces them that there is no hope or help. Their best solution is to destroy themselves.

The actions of Judas parallel those of an Old Testament personality, Ahithophel (see 2 Sam. 15–17). Ahithophel was David's counselor, but he turned traitor and sided with Absalom, David's son, who rebelled against his father and drove him from Jerusalem. When Ahithophel saw that his counsel was not being followed, he went home, "set his house in order, and strangled himself" (2 Sam. 17:23). What David wrote in Psalm 41:9 applies to this event. It is quoted in John 13:18 and referred to in Matthew 26:23 and Luke 22:21.

The psychological and spiritual makeup of Judas had been deteriorating over the previous months. Hidden sin has a way of doing that to the inner person. Satan took over and there could be no resistance. He ended it all by destroying himself, but he only made it worse, for he went to hell to suffer forever. Judas "went out immediately; and it was night" (John 13:30). For Judas, it is still night, and it always will be night.

5. *The son of perdition*

The only jarring note in our Lord's prayer in John 17 is his mentioning of Judas. Judas defiled everything he touched. Even the name that Jesus gave the traitor has an ugly sound to it: the son of perdition. The word "perdition" means destruction, ruin, lostness, waste; it does not mean annihilation. Judas criticized Mary for her waste of the ointment, but he wasted his opportunities, his gifts, and his life. All he left behind was a cemetery with the ominous name "the Field of Blood."

The title "son of perdition" is also used in Scripture to describe the man that Bible scholars call "the Antichrist" (2 Thess. 2:3). This man will be the world's last and greatest dictator, and he will oppose God and Christ to the very end of time. He is called "son of perdition" because it will be his nature to destroy all that is of God. He will seem to succeed for a time, but then Jesus Christ will return and destroy him.

Some teachers think that Judas will be this person, that Judas will be raised from the dead and become a devil incarnate. That there are parallels between Judas and the Antichrist is clear, but these parallels are not necessarily proofs. Satan worked in and through Judas, and Satan will work in and through the Antichrist (2 Thess. 2:9). Both men are called "the son of perdition" because both are involved in ruin and destruction.

What are the practical lessons we can learn from the tragedy of Judas Iscariot? For one thing, Judas is certainly a witness to the person of Jesus Christ. If there had ever been anything questionable about our Lord's life or ministry, Judas would have known about it and could have used it to oppose Jesus. Instead, Judas confesses that Jesus was innocent. Had Jesus been other than what he claimed to be, the Jewish leaders would not have had to pay false witnesses at the trial.

Judas is also a warning against allowing sin to grow in our lives. Sin comes to us as a guest, then becomes a friend, and then becomes a master. Sin grows gradually, but it must be dealt with drastically.

Judas bears witness to the strength of the church. Even though there was a traitor in the midst of the disciple band, he was not able to hinder or destroy the work of God. Wolves in sheep's clothing still try to devour the flock (Matt. 7:15; Acts 20:29–30). The church will have its times of both success and failure, strength and weakness, but the church will prevail.

Judas Iscariot is an example of what can happen when people halfheartedly follow Christ and are not fully trusting him. I fear that our churches may contain many people who are professed Christians but who have never been born again through faith in Jesus Christ. Judas was not committing gross public sins. I am sure he was highly respected by his fellow apostles and by those who followed Jesus. But Judas was a counterfeit; his ministry was only a cover for his sins. We have every reason to believe that, like the other apostles, Judas performed miracles and preached sermons; *yet he died and went to hell.* "Not everyone who says to Me, 'Lord, Lord,' will enter the kingdom of heaven; but he who does the will of My Father who is in heaven. Many will say to Me on that day, 'Lord, Lord, did we not prophesy in Your name, and in Your name cast out demons, and in Your name perform many miracles?' And then I will declare to them, 'I never knew you; depart from Me, you who practice lawlessness'" (Matt. 7:21–23).

Finally, Judas reminds us of how close a person can come to the truth, and to salvation, and finally be lost. If any person ever had the privilege of knowing Christ, it was Judas, but it did not lead him to salvation. Judas heard our Lord preach, saw him perform miracles, and even lived with him and handled his finances; yet Judas Iscariot died a lost soul. John Bunyan expressed this awesome truth at the close of his *Pilgrim's Progress:* "Then I saw that there was a way to hell, even from the gates of heaven. . . ."

Judas went out "and it was night."

"While you have the light, believe in the light, in order that you may become sons of light" (John 12:36).

8
WHAT? IN THE WORLD?

But now I come to Thee; and these things I speak in
the world, that they may have My joy made full in
themselves. I have given them Thy word; and the
world has hated them, because they are not of the
world, even as I am not of the world. I do not ask
Thee to take them out of the world, but to keep them
from the evil one. They are not of the world, even as
I am not of the world.

—John 17:13–16

We have learned that "the world" is an important
concept in John 17. Jesus used the word nineteen times, and he used it in three different
connotations to mean (1) the material creation, as in verse
5; (2) people, as in verse 18; and (3) "the world system"
opposed to God, as in verses 6, 14, and 15.

The Christian has a unique position in life. He lives "in
the world" physically, but he is not "of the world" spiritually. His resources do not come from the evil world system,

but from the Lord. While he is "in the world," he must live *unlike the world* because he must have a ministry to the people who are yet in the world. We are "in the world" to win people "out of the world," and we live with the glorious expectation of being taken from this world when Jesus Christ returns.

In other words, Christians are in enemy territory. "In the world you have tribulation" (John 16:33). "If you were of the world, the world would love its own; but because you are not of the world, but I chose you out of the world, therefore the world hates you" (John 15:19). Like an astronaut in space, or a diver at the bottom of the sea, the Christian is out of his element. And, like the astronaut and diver, the Christian must depend on outside resources if he is going to make it successfully.

Jesus Christ provides for us the spiritual resources we need to overcome the world.

1. *His joy* (v. 13)

It comes a shock to some people that Jesus was a man of joy. We usually hear him described as the "man of sorrows" (Isa. 53:3). Of course, he was a "man of sorrows," but he was also a man filled with the joy of the Lord. He experienced the deepest sorrows and the highest joys as he ministered here on earth. His heart was broken as he saw people destroying themselves with sin. His heart exulted as he saw God at work, saving the lost and making lives new. He had the sorrow of the shepherd seeking the lost sheep, and the joy of the shepherd bringing home the sheep that had been found.

Joy in life is not the absence of sorrow. The Arabs have a motto, "All sunshine makes a desert." If God were to insulate us from sorrow, we would never grow or develop mature character. Heaven is a place of all joy and no sorrow, and hell is a place of all sorrow and no joy. But this present life is a mingling of the two. The fact that Jesus could have joy in the midst of sorrow is proof that we can experience this too.

94

Jesus shares his joy with us. "These things I speak in the world, that they may have My joy made full in themselves" (v. 13). Jesus is always sharing something with us! He shares his love: "Just as the Father has loved Me, I have also loved you; abide in My love" (John 15:9). He shares his peace: "Peace I leave with you; My peace I give to you. . . ." (John 14:27). My love, My joy, My peace—"But the fruit of the Spirit is love, joy, peace. . . ." (Gal. 5:22).

The Christian who experiences the joy of Jesus Christ will not be interested in anything that the world has to offer. When two people fall in love, they are not attracted to anyone else because they are fully satisfied with each other. When a husband or wife starts to find greater joy elsewhere, then trouble begins. Christian joy is a deepening relationship with Jesus Christ, in which we learn more about him and about ourselves. The more we learn about ourselves, the more we see our own needs. But the more we learn about Christ, the more we see how he fully meets those needs. The joy of Jesus Christ does not depend on accidentals or externals. It is something we experience within and the circumstances of the world around us cannot take it away.

Christ gives us joy by *transformation*; the world offers us joy by *substitution*.

If a child breaks a toy, the mother finds another toy for him to play with, or the father goes out and buys a replacement. The child stops his crying, dries his tears, and is happy again. That is joy by substitution. You replace pain with pleasure. But there are some serious problems with this approach to life. For one thing, you may not always be able to get a replacement. Finding a new doll is one thing, but finding a new husband or wife, or replacing a lost arm or leg is quite another. But there is an even greater problem: the philosophy of replacement tends to keep a person immature. It trains a person to live on substitutes.

95

Adults don't usually carry dolls, but they have other toys, and they are quite adept at substitution. If life gets too unbearable, they can always substitute a few drinks for whatever worries them. A few hours of entertainment, perhaps even a "trip" or two on dope will carry them along another day. Sex, spending money, traveling, even a family fight, become substitutes for facing and solving the real problem. People who love by substitution tend to be self-centered and immature. They don't really learn how to deal with sorrow, pain, and disappointment, because they are always turning to a substitute.

Jesus illustrated this principle of *transformation* by using the image of a woman giving birth to a child. "Truly, truly, I say to you, that you will weep and lament, but the world will rejoice; you will be sorrowful, but your sorrow will be turned to joy. Whenever a woman is in travail she has sorrow, because her hour has come; but when she gives birth to the child, she remembers the anguish no more, for joy that a child has been born into the world. Therefore you, too, now have sorrow; but I will see you again, and your heart will rejoice, and no one takes your joy away from you" (John 16:20–22).

This is a perfect illustration of joy that comes through transformation, not through substitution. The same baby that causes the pain also causes the joy. Jesus did not say, "Your sorrow will be replaced by joy." He said, "Your sorrow will be turned to joy." This is transformation. The very thing that brings sorrow to our lives, God transforms to bring joy. The world cannot bring about this kind of spiritual transformation, so the world depends on substitution.

Paul's experience with his thorn in the flesh also illustrates this principle. Just as any of us would do, Paul first prayed that God would remove the thorn. It was a prayer for substitution. God did not remove the thorn, but he did give Paul the grace that he needed to transform that thorn from a weapon into a tool. "Most gladly, therefore, I will rather boast about my weaknesses, that the power of Christ may dwell in me" (2 Cor. 12:9).

This kind of joy cannot be taken from us. Substitute joys are always in danger of being stolen or lost, but sorrows transformed into joys cannot be snatched from us. Why? Because these joys become a part of character. When a Christian learns to transform pain and sorrow into joy, he grows in his character; and that character cannot be taken from him. Only he can destroy his own character.

This principle helps to explain why the Christian has no interest in the substitute pleasures that the world offers. To borrow a popular slogan: we would rather have "the real thing." We expect trials and sorrows, but we know that God will transform these sorrows into joys, if not today, at least when we see him in glory. "Therefore we do not lose heart, but though our outer man is decaying, yet our inner man is being renewed day by day. For momentary, light affliction is producing for us an eternal weight of glory far beyond all comparison" (2 Cor. 4:16–17).

2. *His Word* (v. 14)

Our second resource for overcoming the world is the Word of God. Twice in his prayer, our Lord mentions the gift of the Word (vv. 8 and 14). Since we are living in a deceived and a deceiving world, the possession of the truth of the Word is absolutely essential. It is not our word, but God's Word, that overcomes the deceitfulness of this world system.

The material world was created by the word of God. "And God said, 'Let there be!' And there was!" This is a summary of creation. "By the word of the LORD the heavens were made. . . . For He spoke, and it was done; He commanded, and it stood fast" (Ps. 33:6, 9). The same word that created the universe is also sustaining it (2 Peter 3:7). Everything in the created world, except man, obeys the word of God.

As we have noted before, Christians are in this physical world, but they are not of the "world system" that runs society today. "Society organized without God and against God" might be a good definition of what we mean by "the world system." The believer's citizenship is heavenly and his concerns are for the spiritual and the eternal. The unbeliever's citizenship is earthly, and his concerns are for the physical and material and temporal. The lost sinner looks at spiritual things, cannot understand them, and rejects them. The believer looks at the things of the world (1 John 2:15–17), understands them too well, and rejects them. Hence, there is conflict: the world hates the believer.

The backwoods preacher who defined "status quo" as "the mess we is in" knew what he was talking about. The world system rejects the Word of God and substitutes for it the wisdom of men, the wisdom of this world. The world will tip its hat to God on special occasions, but it will never bow the knee on any occasion. Consequently, we have the status quo—the mess we are in. We have more laws and yet more lawlessness, more knowledge and yet less wisdom, more wealth and yet fewer values, more power and yet greater weakness. As I write these words, our space shuttle has been delayed because of a problem that was finally solved by twenty-five dollars' worth of oil. It's costing taxpayers $3 million a day for that spacecraft to be delayed.

How the Word of God helps us overcome the world is an important thing to know. To begin with, *the Word exposes the world as it truly is.* Lot was impressed with Sodom, but Abraham was not. Why? Because Abraham had his eyes on a better city (Heb. 11:10). Had Lot consulted Abraham, he would have avoided Sodom and stayed with his tent. But the world attracted Lot, so he moved into Sodom, and eventually lost everything. Had Moses been captivated by the prestige and pleasures of Egypt, he would never have left the palace and identified with the Jewish nation. But he saw Egypt as it really was, and he didn't want it. He considered "the reproach of Christ greater riches than the treasures of Egypt; for he was looking to the reward" (Heb. 11:26). Sad to say, the people of Israel did not share his vision and often wanted to go back to Egypt when things got tough. Christians still do that today.

The Bible has nothing good to say about the world system. There is that repeated contrast between "Babylon" and "the heavenly Mount Zion." The wisdom of this world is foolishness to God (1 Cor. 1:18–31). The friendship of this world is enmity with God (James 4:4). The love of the world robs us of the Father's love (1 John 2:15–17). Satan is the prince of this world (John 14:30). The fashion of this world is passing away (1 Cor. 7:31). In fact, the world itself is passing away (1 John 2:17).

The Christian who gets friendly with the world (James 4:4) may find himself *spotted* by the world (James 1:27). A believer rarely plunges into the world; usually, he gradually gets closer and closer, and then falls. Friendship can lead to *loving* the world (1 John 2:15); and when we love the world, we soon get *conformed* to the world (Rom. 12:2). What ought to be separation turns into imitation. The result? We are in danger of being *condemned* with the world and, like Lot, losing everything (1 Cor. 11:32).

Not only does God's Word reveal to us the true nature of the world system, but it also spells out our personal relationship to that system. A true believer will be hated by the world, not because he is offensive, but because he represents Jesus Christ. (Sad to say, there are some Christians who pick fights and become offensive, but that is not what Jesus is talking about.) "If the world hates you," said Jesus, "you know that it has hated Me before it hated you. If you were of the world, the world would love its own; but because you are not of the world, but I chose you out of the world, therefore the world hates you. . . . But all these things they will do to you for My name's sake, because they do not know the One who sent Me" (John 15:18–19, 21).

It is a dangerous thing when the world loves and honors a Christian. Paul declared that he and the other apostles were "a spectacle to the world" (1 Cor. 4:9). The Greek word translated "spectacle" gives us our English word "theater." The verb means "to publicly expose and put to shame." We use the phrase "to make a spectacle of yourself," which carries the same meaning. The world laughs at us and does not take us too seriously, just the way spectators respond to an entertainment in the theater.

Paul also said that he and the apostles were "the scum of the world" (1 Cor. 4:13). The word means "refuse, garbage, off-scouring." Garbage is what you throw away because it is of no value. The world does not value the church, no matter how many speeches worldly people may make about "God" or "truth" or "love." The sooner the Christian believes what the Bible says about the world and his relationship to it, the sooner he will start living in victory over the world. It is impossible for the world system and the Christian to get along with each other (2 Cor. 6:14–7:1). Abraham would not accept even so much as a shoelace from the king of Sodom, lest it affect his walk and give people the idea that he (Abraham) needed the help of the world (Gen. 14:17–24).

The Word of God gives us the dynamic we need to live *in* the world and yet not be *of* the world system. It is our spiritual food and drink, our light to guide us, our companion when people accuse us (Ps. 119:23–24). It is our sword (Eph. 6:17). Like the "blessed man" of Psalm 1, we can meditate on the Word and thereby control our walk and produce fruit for God's glory. When the mind and heart are devoted to the Word of God, there will be given to us the discernment and the power that we need to walk carefully in this present evil age.

The world system, of course, hates the Bible and has tried to destroy it. Satan denied God's Word ("Indeed, has God said . . . ?"), Pharaoh laughed at God's Word, King Jehoiakim burned the Word (Jer. 36), and the world today consigns the Bible to a library shelf with other "ancient religious books." *But the Word of God remains.* And this Word will be here long after the kings and philosophers are gone! The one thing that does more damage to the ministry of the Word than anything else is the careless neglect of the church. The world cannot destroy the Word of God, but the church can defeat the ministry of the Word by careless living and shallow ministry. Unless we read the Word, study it, memorize it, meditate on it, and practice it, we will be overcome by the world instead of being overcomers of the world.

3. *Our identification with Christ* (vv. 14b, 16)

In 1 John 4:17 John makes an astounding statement about Christians and their Lord: "as He is, so also are we in this world." Christ is in heaven and we are on earth, yet we are united in our shared life through the Spirit. Just as the deep-sea diver needs his lifeline above, so the Christian in the world needs a spiritual lifeline to heaven. We are united to Christ: as he is in heaven, so are we in this world.

Of course, this great privilege carries with it tremendous responsibility. We should walk in the light "as He Himself is in the light" (1 John 1:7). We should "walk in the same manner as He walked" (1 John 2:6). We should purify ourselves "as He is pure" (1 John 3:3). We should be righteous "just as He is righteous" (1 John 3:7). One day, when he returns for us, we shall be like him, "because we shall see Him just as He is" (1 John 3:2).

This identification with Christ gives dignity and authority to our lives in the world today. Just as the ambassador to a foreign nation maintains his contact with the home office, so the believer keeps in communion with the glorified Christ. We represent the King of Kings! There is no need to retreat in fear. Rather, let's march forward in faith, "For whatever is born of God overcomes the world; and this is the victory that has overcome the world—our faith" (1 John 5:4). Did you note this tense of that verb? It says "has overcome"—the victory is already won! "In the world you have tribulation, but take courage; I have overcome the world" (John 16:33).

How do we put this "identification" into practice? For one thing, we pray to our Father through the exalted Savior, and draw upon the spiritual power that we find at his throne of grace. Daniel, in Babylon, was surrounded by paganism, false religion, and a world system that was exactly opposite to that which he held; yet Daniel was able to maintain a separated life of service. His secret? Three times a day he went to his room and prayed to God (Dan. 6:10).

Another way we "practice our identification" is by seeking to imitate Christ in our daily walk. While it is true that nobody is saved by trying to imitate Christ, it is also true that seeking to be like him is one evidence that we are saved. "The one who says he abides in Him ought himself to walk in the same manner as He walked" (1 John 2:6). I suggest that we read carefully and often the accounts of our Lord's life given in the four Gospels. In these records we see our Lord as our example. But he is more than an example; for by his spirit we can receive the power to live as he wants us to live. It is more than imitation; it is incarnation. "Christ lives in me" (Gal. 2:20).

Of course, if we begin to live with Jesus Christ as our pattern, the world will treat us the way it treated him. "Remember the word that I said to you, 'A slave is not greater than his master.' If they persecuted Me, they will also persecute you; if they kept My word, they will keep yours also" (John 15:20). Paul calls this experience "the fellowship of His sufferings" (Phil. 3:10). We not only suffer like him, but he suffers with us. We are united in this experience.

It is disturbing to see the false view of the Christian life that is being promoted today. These preachers, singers, and authors talk as though our experience in the world is different from that of the Savior when he was here. They tell us we should be rich, but Jesus was poor. They tell us we should enjoy popularity and acceptance, when he was "despised and forsaken of men" (Isa. 53:3). These popularity promoters say little or nothing about the cross, and the cross that they do preach has little in common with the cross on which Jesus died and by which we have been crucified to the world and the world to us (Gal. 6:14). The marks of spiritual success these days are the very marks of worldliness that we are warned about in Scripture: "the craze for sex, the ambition to buy everything that appeals to you, and the pride that comes from wealth and importance" (1 John 2:16 TLB).

When the world tries to make us conform, we need to remember that we are united with Christ in heaven. "As He is, so also are we in this world" (1 John 4:17). We are representing him on earth and he is representing us in heaven. What he is in heaven we can be on earth, if we will but yield to him and allow his Spirit to work in our lives. The very suffering and persecution that comes to our lives in this world can be used by God to make us more like the Master. In its persecution of God's people, the world only defeats itself; for that suffering only helps to make us more conformed to the image of God's Son.

4. *Christ's intercession on our behalf* (v. 15)

"I do not ask Thee to take them out of the world, but to keep them from the evil one" (v. 15). Our Lord deliberately prayed that the Father would keep us in the world! Why? Because the world needs us, and we need the blessing that comes as we seek to represent Christ in the world.

I have already suggested that there are several false ideas in the minds of some believers regarding their relationship to the world. One is *isolation,* going out of the world. This is the philosophy behind the monastic movement. The great literary giant, Samuel Johnson, once visited a convent in France and conversed with one of the members. "You are not here for love of virtue," he told her, "but from fear of vice." But our Roman Catholic friends are not the only ones who try to escape the world; evangelical Protestants are also guilty. We band together like babes in the woods and try to protect ourselves. We forsake the inner city and establish our citadels in the safe and affluent suburbs (although even the suburbs are not safe anymore). We isolate ourselves from reality, bury our heads in the sand, put on blinders, and pretend that when we open our eyes again we will find ourselves back in the safe and sane fifties.

We are needed in the world, and (in one sense) we need the world. It is by fighting the battles that we grow. It is by remaining on the job that we are able to bring the reconciling message of the cross to an alienated world. Both Joseph and Daniel became great men of God while living in pagan societies. While it is beneficial for us occasionally to "get away," it is not beneficial for us to stay away. Our place is in the world, fighting the world system, and seeking to win people to the Savior.

A second false idea is *insulation*: go ahead and stay in the world, but insulate yourself from its problems and pains. The priest and Levite were willing to walk down the Jericho road, but they were not willing to share the plight of the half-dead man at the side of the road. They were insulated. It is becoming more and more difficult for Christians to maintain compassion in this world simply because we are bombarded with so many emotional stimuli. We no longer hear of "wars and rumors of wars"; we see the actual combat on live TV. Our newspapers are so filled with crime, violence, and corruption that we bypass the front page and turn to the comics or the sports page—and sometimes the crime and violence are even worse there! We have desensitized ourselves. We are no longer our brother's keeper.

But the third false idea is equally as dangerous: *imitation.* "The only way to reach the world is to be like the world," is the philosophy of this camp. As Adam said to Eve when they were leaving the Garden of Eden, "You know, dear, we're living in a time of transition." The popular word "contemporary" can cover a multitude of sins, not the least of which is the blatant imitation of the world. But history convinces us that it was when the church was the least like the world that it did the most to change the world.

Our Lord's heavenly intercession on our behalf centers on our being kept from the evil one, Satan. The devil is the prince of this world and the god of this age. Satan is too strong for us, but he has already been overcome by Christ. If we depend on Christ he will keep us, and the evil one will not be able to touch us (1 John 5:18). The illustration of this truth is found in Exodus 17:8–13. The Amalekites attacked Israel, so Moses sent Joshua out with the army while he went to the top of a hill with the rod of God in his hand. When Moses lifted his hand, Israel began to win the battle. When he dropped his hand, Israel began to fail. So Aaron and Hur held up Moses' hands, and Israel wiped out the enemy. Our Lord intercedes for us in heaven, and his hands will never grow weary. If we look to him by faith, he will give us the victory as we battle against the world.

God's purpose in this heavenly intercession is that he might equip us "in every good thing to do His will, working in us that which is pleasing in His sight. . . ." (Heb. 13:21). He works in us that he might work *through* us.

Instead of being conformed to this world, we are transformed by the renewing of our mind (Rom. 12:2). This is what gives us wisdom and discernment as we face decisions in daily life.

Christ's joy, his Word, our identification with him, and his heavenly intercession for us are the divine resources we have for overcoming the world. Are we using them?

Saints Are Very Special

Sanctify them in the truth; Thy word is truth. As Thou didst send Me into the world, I also have sent them into the world. And for their sakes I sanctify Myself, that they themselves also may be sanctified in truth.

—John 17:17–19

The most popular name today for believers is "Christian," a name that is used only three times in the entire New Testament (Acts 11:26; 26:28; 1 Peter 4:16). In the days of the early church, believers were usually called "disciples" or "saints." The words "saint" and "sanctify" are closely related, so as we study "sanctification" we will discover what it means to be a "saint."

1. *The meaning of "sanctification"*

In both the Old and New Testament, the word "sanctify" means "to be separated from sin and devoted wholly to God." God sanctified the Sabbath day (Gen. 2:3); that is, he set it apart for his own purposes. He also sanctified the firstborn of man and beast (Exod. 13:2). The tabernacle and the temple were "sanctuaries" because they were set apart by God's presence (Exod. 25:8; 2 Chron. 20:8). God sanctified the people of Israel as his own possession (Exod. 31:13). He sanctified the priests to serve in his courts (Lev. 21:8).

But the word need not be related to "religious activities" at all. A pagan army is called "sanctified" in Isaiah 13:3. God had set this army apart for his own use. King Jehu ordered the people to "sanctify a solemn assembly for Baal" (2 Kings 10:20). It is possible even to "sanctify a war" (Joel 3:9). Mount Sinai was "sanctified" when God set bounds about it (Exod. 19:23). The fiftieth year was "sanctified" as the Year of Jubilee (Lev. 25:10). Even the gate of a city can be sanctified (Neh. 3:1)! The sons of Jesse, who were not priests, were sanctified by Samuel when he was seeking the new king (1 Sam. 16:5).

These many references (and there are many more) indicate that sanctification has to do with *position*: someone or something is set apart from common use and devoted entirely to a holy purpose. If you had visited the camp of Israel, you could have rented or purchased any tent in the camp, but not the tabernacle. It was neither for rent nor for sale, because it was set apart for God's use. You could have hired any man in the camp to help you work, but you could not have hired the priests. They were set apart to do God's work. You could have washed your hands in any bowl in the camp; but if you had approached the laver in the tabernacle court, you would have been in trouble. The laver was sanctified, set apart for God's exclusive use.

All saved people are "sanctified in Christ Jesus" (1 Cor. 1:2). Called by his grace, purchased by his blood, and indwelt by his Spirit, we have been set apart from the common things of this world and are devoted to God's exclusive use. The believer's body is the temple of God (1 Cor.

6:19–20); therefore, it is not for rent or for sale. "Present your members [of your body] as slaves to righteousness, resulting in sanctification" (Rom. 6:19). Sanctification is primarily positional. It does not change the nature of the object that is set apart. When the tabernacle was dedicated to God, the laver remained brass, the table remained wood, the skins and cloths did not change, nor did the sockets of silver. Fundamentally, sanctification does not mean "to make something holy" but "to set something apart for holy purposes." Jesus sanctified himself, and yet he certainly did not need to be "made holy." Our Lord's sanctification involved his setting himself apart for the holy purpose of dying for our sins on the cross.

When Paul wrote to the believers in Corinth, he called them "saints" and declared that they had been "sanctified in Christ Jesus" (1 Cor. 1:2). Yet some of the believers in Corinth were living in disobedience to God. There was a four-way split in the church (1 Cor. 1:12). Members were suing each other (1 Cor. 6:1–7). Some of the members were getting drunk at the church fellowship suppers (1 Cor. 11:21). One man was living in open immorality (1 Cor. 5:1–5)! Yet Paul called these people "saints." How can this be? Were they really "sanctified"?

Yes, they were. But they were not practicing their position in Christ. While sanctification is basically a matter of position, it does have its practical aspect. There is such a thing as "progressive sanctification," which simply means that the believer seeks to live daily as one who wholly belongs to God. "Now may the God of peace Himself sanctify you entirely," Paul prayed, "and may your spirit and soul and body be preserved complete, without blame at the coming of our Lord Jesus Christ" (1 Thess. 5:23). John had this same idea in mind when he wrote, "And every one who has this hope fixed on Him purifies himself, just as He is pure" (1 John 3:3).

Let's go back to the camp of Israel. Suppose we discovered a priest roasting a pig on the brazen altar, planning to serve a feast to his friends who had gathered in the tabernacle. We would be shocked. "Isn't that altar dedicated to God?" we would ask. "And isn't the tabernacle dedicated to God? Isn't pork a forbidden food to God's sanctified people?" Suppose the priest replied, "Of course, what you say is true. I am set apart, and so is the tabernacle and everything in it. But that is only a matter of *position*. If I go on with my feast, nothing really changes."

But something does change: God has been robbed of his glory. Positional sanctification must lead to practical sanctification. If we have been set apart for God's exclusive use and for his glory, then we must obey what he commands. Believers *have been sanctified* once and for all in Jesus Christ; but they are also *being sanctified* as they obey the Word, walk in the Spirit, and serve Christ in this world. Separation from sin ought to result in growth in personal holiness. "Therefore, having these promises, beloved, let us cleanse ourselves from all defilement of flesh and spirit, perfecting holiness in the fear of God" (2 Cor. 7:1). "For God has not called us for the purpose of impurity, but in sanctification" (1 Thess. 4:7).

Is it possible for a believer to have some kind of "crisis experience" with the Lord that will make that person completely sinless? I don't think so. As we grow in our spiritual life, we are enabled to conquer sin and temptation more and more; but the tendency and the ability to sin will be with us until we see Christ and are changed to be like him. The *desire* for sin surely ought to diminish as we learn to enjoy the fruits of holiness; but the ability to sin cannot be eradicated. As we mature in the Lord, there ought to be less and less *willful sin* in our lives, the deliberate lawlessness that marks the people of the world. Alas, we still must contend with unrecognized sins that even we may not see.

No wonder David prayed, "Who can discern his errors? Acquit me of hidden faults" (Ps. 19:12). "If we say that we have no sin, we are deceiving ourselves, and the truth is not in us" (1 John 1:8).

Many of God's choicest saints have had crisis experiences that have led them into deeper devotion to the Lord and into a fullness of the Spirit. Paul even went to heaven and back! But Paul confessed himself to be "the very least of all saints" (Eph. 3:8) and the foremost of all sinners (1 Tim. 1:15). The closer we get to the light, the easier it is to see our own defects. It is saints in the shadows who boast about their perfections.

2. *The means of sanctification*

Twice in this passage Jesus states that his people are sanctified "in the truth," that is, through the agency of the Word of God. "Thy word is truth."

There is such a thing as truth. Satan denies this, and naturalistic philosophers agree with him. I recall a college student telling me, "All truth is relative. There is no absolute truth." I asked him if that included the statements he had just made, and to this day he has not given me an answer. Philosophers write learned books to prove that there are no absolutes; yet they use words, and words demand definitions, and definitions imply absolutes. It would seem that the very alphabet that is used to make up the words is to some degree an absolute.

Our God is a God of truth (Ps. 31:5). He is "abundant in lovingkindness and truth" (Ps. 86:15). His works are truth (2 Sam. 7:28). Because God is truth, he is true and faithful in all that he says and does. Therefore, his words are truth. Jesus Christ is "full of grace and truth" (John 1:14). The Holy Spirit is called "the Spirit of truth" (John 14:17).

Because truth is an attribute of God, he can use the truth to sanctify us, to set us apart for holy living. Satan tries to work in our lives through lies (John 8:44), but God works

111

in us through truth (1 Thess. 2:13). God's power is shared with us by means of the Word of truth. When we know and believe God's truth and act upon it, then he is able to work in our lives. Just as the wire carries electricity to the light bulb, so God's truth carries God's power to our lives. We are sanctified in and through God's truth.

God has given us three "editions" of his truth: the Word of God (John 17:17), the Son of God ("I am . . . the truth," John 14:6), and the Spirit of God ("the Spirit is the truth," 1 John 5:7). These three "editions" of truth work together in our lives to sanctify us.

The Word of God is God's truth. "And do not take the word of truth utterly out of my mouth" (Ps. 119:43). "Thou art near, O LORD, and all Thy commandments are truth" (Ps. 119:151). "The sum of Thy word is truth" (Ps. 119:160). Because God's Word is inspired, it is infallible and inerrant in all that it says. "Therefore I esteem right all Thy precepts concerning everything" (Ps. 119:128). When God's Word declares something, we don't debate it; we do it.

Jesus Christ is the truth. He is not simply "true," although that is a valid statement; he is truth. He not only told the truth (John 8:40), but he lived the truth, so that no one was able to accuse him of sin. By his life and ministry, he bore witness to the truth (John 18:37).

The Holy Spirit is truth, because the Holy Spirit is God. The Spirit inspired the Word of truth, and as our teacher, he guides us into all truth (John 16:13). He witnesses of Jesus Christ the truth (John 15:26). There can be no contradiction between the leading of the Spirit and the teaching of the Bible, because both the Spirit and the Word are truth; both point to Jesus Christ.

These three "editions" of truth have been given to us so that we might be completely sanctified, set apart for God's use and God's glory. Jesus Christ is truth—a person I can *love*. The Bible is truth—a book I can *learn*. The Holy Spirit is truth—a person who lives in me to enable me to *live* what I learn in the Word about Jesus Christ. In other words, the whole of the inner person can be controlled by truth. Jesus Christ the truth can capture the love of my heart. The Bible can instruct my mind, and the Spirit can enable my will to obey the truth of God. Heart, mind, and will can be controlled by truth, and this truth sanctifies us.

One of the simple acts that believers perform several times a day is asking God's blessing on the food we eat. This simple act helps us to understand the meaning of sanctification. "For everything created by God is good, and nothing is to be rejected, if it is received with gratitude; for it is sanctified by means of the word of God and prayer" (1 Tim. 4:4–5). How can thanksgiving, the Word of God, and prayer make any difference in roast beef or pork chops? The fact that the Word of God declares that all foods are permissible sets them apart for our enjoyment and use. Our prayer of thanksgiving is evidence that we believe God's Word and accept God's gifts with gratitude. We are therefore able to eat and drink to the glory of God (1 Cor. 10:31). The food is not changed either in nature or quality, but it is still set apart to the glory of God.

God's Word declares that his people are sanctified, set apart for his exclusive use and for his glory. When we believe this and give thanks, we are "practicing our position." When we yield our body for his service, we are putting sanctification into daily practice. Our body does not change, but we are careful how we use our body, where we take it, how we feed it, what we permit it to do. This is what the Bible calls "walking in the truth" (2 John 4).

Any experience that helps us love Christ more, learn the Word of God better, and yield to the control of the Spirit is an experience of sanctification. It might even be a painful experience, but if it makes the truth more meaningful and powerful in our lives, it is a blessed experience. God expects our hearts to love the Word, our minds to learn the Word, and our wills to live the Word. This is how he sets us apart more and more for his glory.

3. The motive for sanctification

We have been sanctified, and we are being sanctified, so that Christ might send us into the world to share the message of the gospel. "As Thou didst send Me into the world, I also have sent them into the world" (v. 18). Sanctification is not for the purpose of displaying our spiritual achievements. It is for the purpose of declaring what God has done for a lost world. Nor is it for the purpose of our own personal enjoyment. Any sanctification that falls short of service and centers only on self is not Bible sanctification. We are sanctified in order that we might be sent. We are set apart from the world so that we might go into the world and rescue lost sinners out of the world.

I have a friend who is investing fifteen years to prepare himself for a highly specialized kind of medical ministry. He has set himself apart for this task, and all of his plans center around this one purpose. He will probably not be able to attend many parties or spend a great deal of money on vacations or the purchasing of various and sundry possessions. But he has set himself apart so that he might be able to serve others. Once his difficult training is ended, he will be able to help people with their complicated physical problems.

Some believers practice a negative kind of sanctification: they are separated *from* sin, but not separated *unto* service. They boast about what they don't do, but they have little to say about what they do accomplish. True sanctification is not only separation from sin; it is also devotion to God, being set apart for his exclusive use. The Pharisees practiced negative separation. They majored on "Thou shalt not!" But they lacked the positive fruit of the Spirit, those God-like qualities that enable us to minister to others. Jesus was "holy, innocent, undefiled, separated from sinners. . . ." (Heb. 7:26), but he was also "a friend of tax-gatherers and sinners" (Matt. 11:19). True sanctification is balanced: we are set apart for God that we might be sent out by God on behalf of others. "Set apart for Me Barnabas and Saul for the work to which I have called them" (Acts 13:2).

Each believer has a ministry in this world, and Jesus Christ gives the authority for that ministry. Just as he was sent by the Father, so we have been sent (see John 10:36). "As the Father has sent Me, I also send you" (John 20:21). We are representing him in this world. "He who receives whomever I send receives Me" (John 13:20).

If you divorce service from sanctification, you will only create problems. The servant must be sanctified—set apart—or his ministry cannot be used of God. Thousands of men in Israel could have performed the same tasks that the priests and Levites performed, but they were not permitted to do so. They had not been anointed with the holy oil and clothed with the special garments. They had not been set apart for the priestly ministry. It was not only a matter of efficiency at the altar, for anybody could have learned to prepare the sacrifices. It was also a matter of calling and consecration. If a man could not prove from the family records that he belonged to the tribe of Levi, he was not permitted to serve as a priest (Ezra 2:59–63).

Our motive for sanctification is service. No matter how holy a person may claim to be, if he is not in some way involved in serving others he is not a sanctified believer.

4. *The model for sanctification*

Jesus Christ is the perfect model for sanctification. "And for their sakes I sanctify Myself. . . ." (v. 19). This statement proves that sanctification does not initially have to do with developing holy character, for Jesus Christ was already holy. "And for their sakes I set myself apart to die on the cross," is what this statement means.

Our Lord is certainly the perfect model of a servant. His disciples were repeatedly debating over which of them was the greatest, while Jesus Christ humbled himself and washed their feet. He had compassion on the needy and ministered to them graciously. He was obedient to the Father's will. He served out of the overflow of a heart of love. His ministry as a servant took him to a cross. "He humbled Himself by becoming obedient to the point of death, even death on a cross" (Phil. 2:8).

Wherever there is true sanctification, there must be service; and wherever there is true service, there must be submission. A servant does not rule. He serves. He submits. The problem Paul faced with the believers in Rome is with us today: "For they all seek after their own interests, not those of Christ Jesus" (Phil. 2:21). Jesus Christ did not think of himself. He sanctified himself "for their sakes."

In the early life of our Lord, we see a perfect example of true sanctification. He was not a recluse. He attended wedding feasts, accepted invitations to dinners, and even played with babies. He worshiped in the synagogues and in the temple. He even mixed with the social outcasts of his day. His enemies called him "a gluttonous man and a drunkard, a friend of tax-gatherers and sinners" (Matt. 11:19). They were exaggerating, of course, but their words indicate that Jesus mixed with people and was not an isolationist.

As we have noted before, true separation is not isolation. Separation is *contact without contamination*. Jesus was both "the friend of sinners" and "separate from sinners." Like a physician he came in contact with infection, but he was not contaminated by it. Nor was he insulated from it. He had compassion on those who were lost and whose lives had been mangled by sin. He felt for them and with them and sought to help them.

True sanctification makes us different from the world, and this difference enables us to minister to the world.

Because Jesus was different, he attracted people. "Now all the tax-gatherers and the sinners [Jews who did not practice the Law] were coming near Him to listen to Him" (Luke 15:1). The Pharisees did not attract this crowd; they repelled them. The Pharisees were isolated and insulated, but Jesus was separated.

There is a danger in our having any other model for our lives besides Jesus Christ. All of us admire the great men and women of history in one way or another, but we cannot always imitate them. When it comes to Jesus Christ, we do more than admire him. We worship him. And in worshiping him, we become more like him. As we become more like him, we become more sanctified, and this means we can serve him better in this world.

Yes, Christians are special people. They are "saints"— set-apart ones, sanctified ones.

And serving ones . . . serving in a world that desperately needs the touch of love and the word of God's grace.

117

10

CHRISTIANS UNITED—OR UNTIED?

I do not ask in behalf of these alone, but for those also who believe in Me through their word; that they may all be one; even as Thou, Father, art in Me, and I in Thee, that they also may be in Us; that the world may believe that Thou didst send Me. And the glory which Thou hast given Me I have given to them; that they may be one, just as We are one; I in them, and Thou in Me, that they may be perfected in unity, that the world may know that Thou didst send Me, and didst love them, even as Thou didst love Me. Father, I desire that they also, whom Thou hast given Me, be with Me where I am, in order that they may behold My glory, which Thou hast given Me; for Thou didst love Me before the foundation of the world.

—John 17:20–24

In this closing portion of his prayer, our Lord emphasizes the matter of spiritual unity. He had mentioned it before (v. 11), but now it becomes the burden of his prayer. Perhaps he had Psalm 133:1 in mind: "Behold, how good and how pleasant it is for brothers to dwell together in unity!" You would expect brothers to get along with each other, but alas, sometimes they do not. All of us need to heed Joseph's advice to his brothers, "Do not quarrel on the journey" (Gen. 45:24).

Bible history and church history bear record to the sad fact that believers do not always get along with each other. Even our Lord's disciples argued with one another, and Jesus was right there with them! Paul and Barnabas had a falling out over John Mark, and some of the New Testament churches broke Paul's heart with their disputes and divisions. Spiritual unity is a rare commodity. No wonder our Lord included it in his prayer for his church.

We must understand that our Lord's prayer for unity cannot be fulfilled in some man-made organization. Putting all religious groups together, regardless of what they profess to believe, will not solve the problem. Disregarding doctrine and watering everything down to the least common denominator is not what Jesus had in mind. Doctrine is an essential part of unity. There is not only "one Lord," but there is also "one faith" (Eph. 4:5), and we are to "contend earnestly for the faith which was once for all delivered to the saints" (Jude 3).

The unity Christ has in mind is a *spiritual* unity that comes from within. He compares this unity with the oneness of the Father and the Son in their relationship in the Trinity. While true believers may disagree on some points of interpretation, they are one in Christ. It has been my privilege to minister to many different evangelical groups in different parts of the world, and I have always felt right at home. I probably could have started some kind of disagreement by bringing up minor matters that even the godliest saints may not agree on, but I felt it was better to major on what we did agree on.

A Baptist pastor I know invited a well-known preacher, a Presbyterian, to conduct a Bible conference. The guest preacher's first sermon was on infant baptism! Another pastor friend of mine invited a famous Bible teacher into his pulpit, and the guest preached a long sermon that contradicted that church's views on prophecy. There are times and places when it is right to share your convictions, but there are also times when courtesy demands that we promote unity and not division.

Our Lord gives us every encouragement for spiritual unity by reminding us of the bonds that tie us together.

1. *We trust the same Savior* (vv. 20–21a).

It is this faith in Christ that makes a person a Christian, and this is the *only* way to be saved. The gift of eternal life comes through knowing God, through faith in Jesus Christ (John 17:3). Jesus Christ is the only Savior (John 14:6; Acts 4:12), because Jesus Christ is God. There can be no spiritual oneness—fellowship, partnership—with those who deny the deity of Christ. Our oneness is in him; if he is not God and Savior, there can be no unity.

"What do you think about the Christ, whose son is He?" (Matt. 22:42) is still life's most important question. The way we answer that question determines where we spend eternity. Some religious people claim that Jesus Christ was only a gifted Jewish teacher, or perhaps a religious martyr for a lost cause. Others say that he was a "son of God" in the same way each of us is "a son of God" (whatever that means). But unless a person affirms that Jesus Christ is God, I cannot have spiritual fellowship and unity with him. We might be able to serve on a PTA committee together, but we could never have spiritual fellowship. The word "fellowship" means "to have in common." The center of our Christian unity is the person of Jesus Christ, and unless we share his life, we have nothing spiritual in common.

Something else is important: the work of Jesus Christ on the cross. "I glorified Thee on the earth, having accomplished the work which Thou hast given Me to do" (John 17:4). You cannot easily separate the person and the work of Jesus Christ, for they go together. He is the only one who could have accomplished the work of redemption for a lost world. The cross declares that man is a sinner and that he cannot save himself. The cross also declares that God loves sinners and that salvation is accomplished once and for all. To make our Lord's death anything other than a sacrifice for sins is to deny both his person and his work. He said, "Just as the Son of Man did not come to be served, but to serve, and to give His life a ransom for many" (Matt. 20:28 NASB).

Because we share his life, we can experience spiritual unity. We may not agree on every detail of doctrinal interpretation, but if we know him and share his life, we can experience unity. It is possible even to disagree without being disagreeable. St. Augustine said: "In essentials, unity; in non-essentials, liberty; in all things, charity." One day we shall all "attain to the unity of the faith" (Eph. 4:13). Meanwhile, we must love one another for Jesus' sake and try not to major on minors. It is sad to see Sunday school classes and churches dispute and divide over matters that are relatively unimportant. If each of us would only learn to regard others as more important than ourselves (Phil. 2:3), we would have an easier time promoting spiritual unity.

2. *We bear the same witness to the world* (v. 21b).

Twice in this prayer, the Savior mentions the church's witness to the lost world: "that the world may believe that Thou didst send Me" (v. 21); "that the world may know that Thou didst send Me" (v. 23). We live before the keen eyes of a watching world that is only too quick to detect hypocrisy and defects in the church.

In one of the churches I pastored, we were repeatedly praying for the husband of one of the members. He was a good man who never hindered his wife from attending church services, but he himself wanted nothing to do with the Savior. I often visited him and witnessed to him, but seemed to get nowhere. I wondered why. Then I discovered that some of the men in the church who worked with him were prone to talk about church problems, and my unsaved friend was getting all the negative reports. It was no wonder he had little interest in the things of the Lord! In the eyes of God, the church is not divided. "There is one body" (Eph. 4:4). But in the eyes of a lost world the church is divided, and not only divided, but involved in some serious family feuds. The competition among churches and other Christian groups is a dishonor to the name of Christ. Especially distasteful are those groups who claim to have *all* the truth. They believe they are the only ones who are right and who are doing the will of God on earth. The world laughs at this and refuses to take the gospel message seriously. We live in a divided world, and the church needs to bear witness to the spiritual unity that we have in Jesus Christ. "We have enough problems of our own," says the thinking unbeliever. "Why get involved in the church and have even more problems?"

It is obvious that this unity our Lord prayed about is not simply internal and personal. It is big enough and strong enough for the world to see. We don't have to form a new organization or put on a promotional program. When Christians love each other and bear witness together, the world will see it. Jesus did not pray for a temporary, artificial uniformity that would impress people. He prayed for a permanent and sincere unity that would bear witness to Jesus Christ and prove to the world that he was sent by God. There is variety in the church, so we don't want uniformity of method or organization. Nor do we want the kind of crowd psychology that develops around a strong and gifted leader. We want Christians who love each other because they love Christ and share his life.

Jesus assures us in this prayer that some will believe because of our witness (v. 20). What an encouragement this statement must have been to Peter when he faced that crowd at Pentecost! Or to Paul when he traveled to pagan cities with the gospel message! We are not the fainting promoters of a lost cause. We are the triumphant heralds of the King of kings, and he has assured us that some will believe. In fact, in this prayer, our Lord has already prayed for those we are going to win!

We have another guarantee of success: he has given us his word. "So shall My word be which goes forth from My mouth; it shall not return to Me empty, without accomplishing what I desire, and without succeeding in the matter for which I sent it" (Isa. 55:11). Note that Jesus called the message "their word." The witness of God's Word must be personalized in our lives. We do not all take the same approach, even though we all proclaim the same Good News of salvation. The Word reveals itself in and through our lives in just the ways that God has ordained. This explains why we go through the various experiences of life, for each experience helps us to share the Word in a new way.

It is good to know that we do not witness alone. Sometimes we get "the Elijah complex" and think that we are the only faithful ones left in the world; but others are praying and witnessing, too. In fact, God usually uses many laborers to reap his harvest: "that he who sows and he who reaps may rejoice together" (John 4:36). When we get to heaven, we are going to be amazed to see how God used even our chance remarks to bring people to a knowledge of salvation.

When it comes to our witness to a lost world, there must be no competition among God's servants. We must never say or do anything that would make it difficult for another Christian to witness or to win a lost soul. We may not always agree with the methods of some saints, but we must help them spread the message. "Now may the God who gives perseverance and encouragement grant you to be of the same mind with one another according to Christ Jesus; that with one accord you may with one voice glorify the God and Father of our Lord Jesus Christ" (Rom. 15:5–6).

3. *We share the same glory* (vv. 22, 24).

When Moses dedicated the tabernacle and Solomon dedicated the temple, the glory of God moved in. The presence of God's glory made Israel a unique people (see Rom. 9:4–5). When God guided Israel in the wilderness, it was his glory that led the way. These twelve distinctive tribes were united by the glory of God.

Each individual Christian is God's temple, and the glory of God dwells within. Christ has already given us the glory, even though the full manifestation of this glory awaits the return of the Savior (Rom. 8:19). The presence of God's Spirit within marks a person as a true believer (Rom. 8:9). He has the glory, and one day we will share the glory of Christ and have a glorified body.

One of the major causes of divisions among believers is majoring on the externals and neglecting or ignoring the internals. We build on accidentals, not on essentials. Churches have been built on the basis of the ministry of a strong personality, and when that leader left, the church fell apart. Fellowships have been organized to promote some special doctrine or to fight some enemy, and when the cause vanished the fellowship melted away. At the turn of the century, many churches were organized on the basis of ethnic background. When the second and third generations came along, however, they did not want to be identified with "the old country," and the churches began to decay.

Whenever you meet another Christian, keep in mind that he shares with you the same glory that Christ gave his disciples. His skin may be a different color; he may live in

125

a different section of town; he may have some approaches to worship that you are not accustomed to. But if he has the glory within and he is seeking to glorify God, you two can share a common fellowship and witness.

Those of us who are privileged to travel a bit realize that Christians are not all the same around the world. They belong to the same Savior and believe the same gospel, but they do not always express their faith in the same manner. In some parts of the world, evangelical ministers wear clerical collars. I recall being criticized by a church member because I fellowshiped with a converted Anglican minister who wore clerical garb! "That man wears his collar backwards!" this member sputtered. "That brands him as a liberal!" Does it really?

What a difference it would make in our personal relationships with other believers if we would try to look beyond the externals and remember that we share the same glory within. We do not need to manufacture unity; it is already there. Our job is to be "diligent to preserve the unity of the Spirit in the bond of peace" (Eph. 4:3). And it takes diligence! One wrong word, one misinterpreted action, one selfish motive, and the enjoyment of unity is gone. If we Christians would work as hard at maintaining unity as we do at attacking it, we would all be happier and holier people. If we would stop worrying about glorifying ourselves or the group we belong to and start being concerned about glorifying Christ, we would experience the kind of oneness that Jesus prayed for in this prayer.

Not only do we have the glory now, but we shall see his glory when we go to heaven (v. 24). The fact that we are going to be in heaven together one day ought to encourage us to try to get along with each other today. It is a well-known fact that John Wesley and George Whitefield disagreed on doctrine and even published open letters in the newspapers. Somebody asked Whitefield if he expected to see Wesley in heaven. "No, I don't," said Whitefield. "For John Wesley will be so close to the throne of God, and I so far back, that I will not see him." A gracious attitude, indeed, but it is still too bad that these gifted men could not unite their hearts while on earth.

The next time we are tempted to declare war on a brother or sister, let's remember that we are going to be in heaven together. The hope of heaven ought to motivate us to love one another. Is hope a motive for love? Paul thought that it was. Paul was thankful for the Colossian believers, "praying always for you, since we heard of your faith in Christ Jesus and the love which you have for all the saints; *because of* the hope laid up for you in heaven. . . ." (Col. 1:3–5, italics mine). There is something about going home together that unites our hearts in love. Even the Lord Jesus connected his glory with the Father's love: "for Thou didst love Me before the foundation of the world" (v. 24).

When I was a young pastor, I was perplexed at the hostile attitudes displayed by relatives of the deceased at funerals. During the service, they would sit placidly together, but afterward they would sometimes argue and fight. Even some of our best church members would "fall out" with each other after a funeral. Then I discovered that bereavement often opens up old wounds and creates a feeling of guilt. Hostility is sometimes guilt turned inside out. Sometimes the estate is a factor. ("Where there's a will, there are relatives.") More than once I have had to be a peacemaker in a home after we had buried a loved one.

It would seem that just knowing a loved one is in heaven would encourage family members to love each other, for as believers, they, too, will be in heaven someday. I sometimes wonder if, at the judgment seat of Christ, there will not be some adjustments made in the relationships of Christians. Perhaps some of us will have to make some apologies!

One day a gentleman in his sixties walked into my office and asked me if I would conduct his wedding. He and his bride were both Christians. "I suppose you are a widower and your bride is a widow?" I said. He smiled and replied: "She and I were married to each other years ago. We had a silly spat and impulsively got a divorce. Neither of us remarried. But the longer we lived, and the closer we got to the end of life, the more we realized that we had been foolish. That's why we want to get remarried." It was one of the sweetest weddings I have ever conducted.

We share the same glory now, and we shall behold the same glory in heaven. We are united in his glory. The hope of heaven ought to bind us together as the family of God. "There is one body, and one Spirit, just as also you were called in one hope of your calling" (Eph. 4:4).

Can every true believer be sure he is going to heaven? Of course, he can! Jesus prayed that the Father would take us to heaven and the Father always answers the prayers of his beloved Son. Every time a Christian dies the prayer of verse 24 is answered and the soul of that Christian goes to heaven. In fact, Jesus used a very strong word in this request: "I desire." There could be no question. God answers this prayer and believers go to heaven.

4. *We enjoy the same love* (v. 23).

The Father loved the Son from before the foundation of the world (v. 24). The Father also loves his children even as he loved Christ. "For the Father Himself loves you, because you have loved Me" (John 16:27). "Just as the Father has loved Me, I have also loved you; abide in My love" (John 15:9). "If anyone loves Me, he will keep My word; and My Father will love him, and We will come to him, and make Our abode with him" (John 14:23).

The motivation for unity is not only hope, but also love. "Behold, how they love one another!" was the world's testimony to the early church. "And all those who had believed were together" (Acts 2:44). It is significant that *love* is an important element in Ephesians 4:1–16, that major passage dealing with Christian unity. "With all humility and gentleness, with patience, showing forbearance to one another in love" (Eph. 4:2). "But speaking the truth in love. . . ." (Eph. 4:15) "causes the growth of the body for the building up of itself in love" (Eph. 4:16). Someone has said, "Love is the circulatory system of the body." How true! *Truth* and *love* work together to build the body of Christ. It has well been said that truth without love is brutality ("I'm going to tell you the truth whether you like it or not!"), and love without truth is hypocrisy. I have preached in churches where there was a great deal of truth, but very little love; the atmosphere was cold and defensive. I have also preached in assemblies where there seemed to be love, but there was a glaring absence of Bible doctrine; their "love" was only sentimentality, a masquerade put on for the occasion. The body grows in an atmosphere of truth and love. The ministry of the Word must be truthful and loving. The personal relationships of the church members must reflect truth and love. The moment that lies and selfishness enter, unity is in danger of being destroyed. How tragic it is when pastors and other church leaders resort to lies, politics, scheming, and selfish actions. "Speaking the truth in love" is still God's way to build his church.

Love is not something that we manufacture. We can learn to like people, but only God can enable us to love people. True Christian love involves concern for one another and ministry to one another. The test of *truth* and *love* is not always in the public services of the church, but in the committee meetings where members meet head-on! All of us are sure of God's will for the church, and none of us is willing to change his mind! How often I have thought of Oliver Cromwell's message to the people of Scotland, "I beseech you, in the bowels of Christ, think it possible you may be mistaken." Unfortunately, they did not think it possible, and the result was war of brother against brother. True Christian love does not say, "Peace at any price." James 3:17 makes it clear that "the wisdom from above is first pure, then peaceable. . . ." To compromise on the basic doctrines of the faith does not produce peace; it only means surrender to the enemy without a battle. We love one another because we love Christ and his truth. We do not simply "speak in love," we "speak *the truth* in love."

As we mature in the Lord, we find that it is possible to disagree without being disagreeable. Every family knows what it means to disagree, talk things over, practice give and take, and reach an amicable solution. Where there is love we can afford to disagree, for love encourages an open atmosphere of sharing and growing. Where there is truth we need not fear open communication, for truth ministered in love always builds us up.

These bonds of spiritual unity can only be given and strengthened by the Holy Spirit of God. It is he who reveals Jesus Christ to us and glorifies him. It is the Spirit who energizes us for our witness to the world (Acts 1:8). It is he who has deposited the glory within us and made us the temple of God. It is he who produces the fruit of love in our hearts and who causes the love of God to be "poured out within our hearts" (Rom. 5:5).

Without the Spirit, there can be no spiritual unity.

When you and I are filled with the Spirit and walking in the Spirit, then there can be true spiritual unity.

Be "diligent to preserve the unity of the Spirit in the bond of peace" (Eph. 4:3).

11

THE WORLD, THE CHURCH, AND THE FATHER

O righteous Father, although the world has not
known Thee, yet I have known Thee; and these have
known that Thou didst send Me; and I have made
Thy name known to them, and will make it known;
that the love wherewith Thou didst love Me may be
in them, and I in them.

—John 17:25–26

Many of us, when we get to the end of our prayers,
commit one or both of two common blunders.
We either repeat ourselves, just in case God
didn't hear us the first time, or we ramble from statement
to statement like a frantic mosquito looking for a place to
land.

When our Lord reached the end of his High Priestly
prayer, he made no requests. He simply reaffirmed that the
Father was righteous and that the Son had done in the
world what the Father sent him to do: reveal truth and love.
These are the two primary themes of these closing verses:
truth and *love.* The world knows little of either one, but the

Son has made it possible for his church to enjoy truth and love.

We will consider each of these themes separately, and then join them together to see how they relate to each other.

1. *Truth*

"What is truth? said jesting Pilate; and would not stay for an answer." So wrote Francis Bacon in a famous essay. I am not so sure that Pilate was jesting; his predicament was too serious for that. "What is truth?" was, and still is, a common question among philosophers and others who look beyond bread, circuses, and television entertainment.

Our Lord makes it clear that the world does not know truth. The world certainly knows a great deal of facts. Knowledge is multiplying so rapidly that we cannot keep up with it. Technical information is doubling every ten years, the experts tell us. There are now over 100,000 technical journals published in the world. About 700,000 new titles are published around the world each year. We are in the midst of a knowledge explosion.

But *knowledge* and *wisdom* are two different commodities. The scientist who can split the atom cannot keep his family together at home. The professor who can explain microbiology does not understand his own teenage children. The banker who manages millions of dollars loses his values, and the popular recording star who knows how to "turn on" an audience turns off her own life by taking too many pills. Henry David Thoreau was right: we have improved means to unimproved ends.

The world lacks wisdom because it lacks truth, and truth comes from knowing the Father. After all, God made this world, and if we are going to understand what this world is all about we must get acquainted with the Creator. Man is made in the image of God, and man cannot really know himself unless he knows the Father, the divine original. God's fingerprints are on creation and his footprints are

132

seen in human history; but both creation and history remain an enigma until we know God. The sad fact is this: the world chooses *not* to know God. The record is given in Romans 1:18–32. "For even though they knew God, they did not honor Him as God, or give thanks; but they became futile in their speculations, and their foolish heart was darkened. Professing to be wise, they became fools" (Rom. 1:21–22). The biblical record of man's history is not that of evolution, but devolution: man started at the top and sinned his way down.

Through creation around him and conscience within him, man has every evidence of the existence, power, and wisdom of God. Paul affirmed to the Greek philosophers at Mars Hill, "He Himself gives to all life and breath and all things; and He made from one, every nation of mankind to live on all the face of the earth, having determined their appointed times, and the boundaries of their habitation, that they should seek God, if perhaps they might grope for Him and find Him, though He is not far from each one of us; for in Him we live and move and exist. . . ." (Acts 17:25–28). This statement covers just about everything. He is the God of creation, of history (he determines the times), of geography (he sets the boundaries), and of our personal lives. Paul seemed to think that the evidence was obvious enough for even a philosopher to see.

Why, then, does the world not see?

Pride is one cause of the world's spiritual blindness. God has hidden these things from the wise and revealed them to babes. The truly wise man knows that he does not know. He also admits that there is more than one route to knowledge, and that the spiritual world, which is just as real as the physical, is not accessible to microscopes or computers. "The fear of the LORD is the beginning of knowledge. . . ." (Prov. 1:7). Alas, "There is no fear of God before their eyes" (Rom. 3:18).

133

Another blindfold that keeps the world from seeing truth is *willful sin*. "And this is the judgment," said Jesus, "that the light is come into the world, and men loved the darkness rather than the light; for their deeds were evil. For everyone who does evil hates the light, and does not come to the light, lest his deeds should be exposed" (John 3:19–20). Evangelist Billy Sunday used to say that a sinner cannot find God for the same reason that a criminal cannot find a policeman—he's not looking! "If any man is willing to do His will, he shall know of the teaching. . . ." (John 7:17). Obedience is still the organ of spiritual knowledge.

A third cause of spiritual darkness is *the blinding work of Satan*. "And even if our gospel is veiled," explained Paul, "it is veiled to those who are perishing, in whose case the god of this world has blinded the minds of the unbelieving, that they might not see the light of the gospel of the glory of Christ, who is the image of God" (2 Cor. 4:3–4). One of Satan's most successful blindfolds is *religion without Christ*. If he can get a person to cultivate self-righteousness and religious morality, the adversary has that person at the gates of hell. The Pharisees in our Lord's day are classic examples. The apostle Paul, a Pharisee, had to lose his religion in order to go to heaven.

In contrast to the spiritual ignorance of the world is the spiritual intelligence of the church. The Son knows the Father, and he has revealed the Father to those who have trusted him. "All things have been handed over to Me by My Father; and no one knows the Son, except the Father; nor does anyone know the Father, except the Son, and anyone to whom the Son wills to reveal Him" (Matt. 11:27). That dramatic statement is then followed by one of the most gracious invitations recorded in the Bible: "Come to Me, all who are weary and heavy-laden, and I will give you rest" (Matt. 11:28). Two facts are obvious: those who do not know the Father are weary and burdened; and those who want to know the Father (and thus get rid of their burdens) can do so by coming to the Son by faith. The invitation is for all.

Need we remind ourselves of the importance of knowing the Father? If a person does not know the Father, that person is lost and condemned forever. Eternal life means knowing the Father through the Son, Jesus Christ (John 17:3). As we have seen, this is not a mere intellectual knowledge or an assent to certain doctrinal statements. It is a personal experience of God's life within us. By trusting Jesus Christ and yielding to him, we enter into a living union with God and share his life. Apart from this, there is no salvation.

God reveals himself in Jesus Christ, and he reveals himself to those who admit their need and humble themselves. "But to this one will I look," says the Lord, "to him who is humble and contrite of spirit, and who trembles at My word" (Isa. 66:2). Paul learned a great deal of theology when he sat at the feet of Gamaliel, but he met God personally when he fell at the feet of Jesus and cried, "What shall I do, Lord?" (Acts 22:10).

God's people know that Jesus Christ is the Son of God, sent from the Father. If a person is wrong about the person of Jesus Christ, he will be wrong about everything else that relates to Jesus Christ, including salvation. We are not saved from our sins by a great teacher or a good example. We are saved by a Redeemer who died for us on the cross. Furthermore, God's people know the Father's name. "I have made Thy name known to them" (John 17:26). As we have seen, "Thy name" simply means "Thy nature," what God is like. The better we know God, the better we understand his Word, his world, and ourselves, for we are made in his image. Life without God is life without meaning.

But this intimate revelation of God is not a past event, recorded in history and embalmed for our admiration. *Jesus*

135

Christ continues to reveal the Father to us. This revelation is found in his Word, and the teacher is the Holy Spirit of God. "But the Helper, the Holy Spirit, whom the Father will send in My name, He will teach you all things, and bring to your remembrance all that I said to you" (John 14:26).

What the Spirit teaches us, of course, depends on our own spiritual condition. "I have many things more to say to you, but you cannot bear them now" (John 16:12). As we obey what we know, God teaches us what we need to know. It is possible to grow in knowledge about the Bible and yet not grow in knowledge of God. It is the difference between analyzing a recipe or eating a meal, or the difference between looking at a photograph of a person and then meeting the person.

God's revelation of himself in nature, in the Bible, and in Jesus Christ is a completed revelation, but there is always something new to learn. We are not seeking *for* truth; we are seeking *into* truth. We are not asking for some new revelation, but we are asking the Spirit for new *illumination* into what God has already revealed. "But when He, the Spirit of truth, comes, He will guide you into all the truth. . . ." (John 16:13). He will not push us; he will guide us. Learning about God involves our willingness to learn. The Spirit waits to guide us.

Phillips Brooks once said that the purpose of life is the building of character through truth. We have that truth in Jesus Christ, recorded in the Word of God, taught by the Spirit of God. The world is ignorant of this truth, but believers are privileged to know the truth and experience it in daily life.

2. *Love*

Our Lord is concerned with love as well as truth: "that the love wherewith Thou didst love Me may be in them, and I in them." Since God is a God of truth and love, truth and love must go together. Satan is a liar, and therefore he is a murderer and a destroyer. If we are growing in our personal appropriation of truth, we must express it in love. It is not enough only to grow in knowledge; we must also grow in grace (2 Peter 3:18).

Jesus makes the astounding statement that the Father's love for the Son can be in us. The Father loves us even as he loves the Son (John 17:23). He loved the Son from before the foundation of the world (John 17:24). Incredible as it seems, believers share in the eternal love that the Father has for the Son! "The love of God has been poured out within our hearts through the Holy Spirit who was given to us" (Rom. 5:5).

Keep in mind that one of the emphases in this prayer is the believer's victory over the world. It is this experience of the Father's love that helps us to overcome the world. "If any one loves the world, the love of the Father is not in him" (1 John 2:15). "Therefore whoever wishes to be a friend of the world makes himself an enemy of God" (James 4:4).

Jesus is hinting here at a marvelous truth that is later developed in detail by the apostle Paul in his epistles: *the wonder of the indwelling Christ*. We are "in Christ" and Christ is "in us," and this means we are "in the Father" as well. Our spiritual union with Christ is a fact, not a feeling, although there are certainly times of rapturous fellowship through the Spirit. Just as husband and wife love each other with a deeper and sweeter love, a love that is expressed in many intimate and practical ways, so the believer enjoys many different experiences of the love of God.

It is this living and loving union with Christ that enables us to overcome the world and accomplish God's will. "Christ lives in me!" declared Paul (Gal. 2:20). "Now to Him who is able to do exceeding abundantly beyond all that we ask or think, according to the power that works within us" (Eph. 3:20). "I can do all things through Him who strengthens me" (Phil. 4:13). His life provides the power, and his love provides the motive. We are branches of the true vine. We do not manufacture blessings; we bear fruit (John 15:1–6).

How do we cultivate this love? By fellowship with the Savior. Just as a husband and wife grow in their love by talking together, listening, spending time together, and seeking to please each other, so the believer grows in his love for Christ. (The experiences of the bride recorded in the Song of Solomon illustrate this truth.) In my early Christian life, I used to be somewhat embarrassed singing some of the hymns about love; but now I sing them with understanding and delight. I hope I do more than sing them. I hope I also *experience* them in my own personal communion with the Savior.

Truth has to do with doctrine; love has to do with dynamic. Love is the greatest force for good in the world. "Beloved, let us love one another, for love is from God; and every one who loves is born of God and knows God" (1 John 4:7). If we Christians do not learn to love *one another*, how will we ever learn to love lost souls or even love our enemies? God's love was (and is) so great that he gave his Son. Christ's love was (and is) so great that he gave his life on the cross. We share in that love through the indwelling Holy Spirit. How can we claim to be "born again" and still refuse to love God's children? "We know that we have passed out of death into life, because we love the brethren. He who does not love abides in death. Everyone who hates his brother is a murderer; and you know that no murderer has eternal life abiding in him" (1 John 3:14–15).

Christian love is not promiscuous; it exercises discernment. "And this I pray, that your love may abound still more and more in real knowledge and all discernment, so that you may approve the things that are excellent [margin: distinguish between the things which differ], in order to be sincere and blameless until the day of Christ" (Phil. 1:9–10). I once made a pastoral visit to a man who was suffering with a brain tumor, and the man bitterly attacked me with unkind criticism. "Don't take it too seriously," explained the man's wife. "Often, people with brain tumors love those they ought to hate and hate those they ought to love. He can't help it." But Christians *can* help it! The Holy Spirit can give us the discernment we need.

Christian love is practical; it expresses itself in words and deeds. "God so loved the world that He gave. . . ." (John 3:16). Someone has defined "sentiment" as "feeling without responsibility." It is easy to get sentimental about the needs of people, and to have a "feeling" down inside, and yet do nothing to meet those needs. Christian love is not simply a matter of the emotions; it is also a matter of the will. Christian love means that we treat other people the way God treats us. God has forgiven us, so we forgive others. God meets our needs, so we try to help meet the needs of others. God listens when we speak to him, so we listen when people speak to us. Christian love is seen in our attitudes and our actions; otherwise what we think is "love" is only shallow sentiment.

3. *Truth and love*

Jesus united truth and love in his person and in his teaching. His love was expressed in truth, and he spoke the truth with love. Truth and love together are necessary for spiritual growth. "But speaking the truth in love, we are to grow up in all aspects unto Him, who is the head, even Christ" (Eph. 4:15).

It is easy to detect those Christians who have a great deal of truth, but who are short on love. Their faith is expressed primarily in words. They are "great Bible students" and can outline the books and chart the ages. But they are difficult to get along with, and the truth they know (or think they know) is not a tool to build with; it is a weapon to fight with. They love to argue!

Truth needs love, for truth without love tends to make a person proud. "Knowledge makes arrogant, but love edifies" (1 Cor. 8:1). Truth alone can be destructive, but love enables truth to build us up. When truth is shared in love (even if truth hurts) it helps us in the end. "Faithful are the wounds of a friend, but deceitful are the kisses of an enemy" (Prov. 27:6). A child thinks that everyone who kisses him is a friend and that everyone who spanks him is an enemy, but a mature person knows better. Sometimes the truth must wound us before it can heal us, but if we are wounded in love, the healing will soon come.

This fact helps us to understand why some ministries of the Word are divisive and destructive. There is truth, but the truth is not shared in love. Or, there is love, but that love is not based on truth. There must be a balance. If love lacks spiritual discernment, it will tear down instead of build up. If truth lacks love, it will destroy. "Speaking the truth in love" must always be our aim.

Truth and love help to unite the mind and heart of the believer. The mind grows by taking in; the heart grows by giving out. As the mind receives truth, and as the heart shares love, we grow to become more like our Master. Truth is not a toy to play with or a weapon to fight with (unless we are fighting the enemy), but it is a tool to build with. Nothing builds and balances the Christian life like "speaking the truth in love." Nothing purifies and strengthens a home or a church family like "speaking the truth in love." Truth and love are the circulatory system of the body of Christ that help it to grow and glorify God.

There are times when truth is attacked and the dedicated Christian must take his stand, but even then, he must do it in love. Christ is our example in this: "leaving you an example for you to follow in His steps, who committed no sin, nor was any deceit found in His mouth; and while being reviled, He did not revile in return; while suffering, He uttered no threats, but kept entrusting Himself to Him who judges righteously" (1 Peter 2:21–23). "But let everyone be quick to hear, slow to speak and slow to anger; for the anger of man does not achieve the righteousness of God" (James 1:19–20).

It is our personal communion with Christ through the Word that enables us to balance truth and love. "He who has My commandments and keeps them, he it is who loves Me; and he who loves Me shall be loved by My Father, and I will love him, and will disclose Myself to him. . . . If anyone loves Me, he will keep My word; and My Father will love him, and We will come to him, and make Our abode with him" (John 14:21, 23). It is love that gives dynamic to truth, and it is truth that gives discernment and discipline to love. Both are the beautiful fruit of our intimate fellowship with the Father and the Son, and our obedience to what he tells us in the Word. "If you love Me, you will keep My commandments" (John 14:15).

The Word of God must constantly be "made flesh" in our lives as we obey his will. It is not enough for us merely to *know* the truth, or to argue for it or defend it; we must live it. D. L. Moody used to say that all Bibles should be bound in shoe leather! The Christian is a "living Bible," a flesh-and-blood translation of the Word. "You are a letter of Christ . . . written not with ink, but with the Spirit of the living God, not on tablets of stone, but on tablets of human hearts" (2 Cor. 3:3).

It is sad to see how some Christians have polarized truth and love. Instead of uniting these qualities, they have separated them. Some Christians are so concerned with truth (or their version of truth) that they will fight, accuse, attack, malign, and do everything short of murder to destroy those who disagree with them. Others are so concerned with love (or what they think is love) that they water down the truth, compromise, and sell out to the enemy. Both extremes are wrong. Truth is a mighty weapon, but it is even mightier when it is united with love. Love is an invincible power, but it is even greater when it is united with truth.

Blessed are the balanced, for they shall be like the Lord Jesus Christ!

12
PRIORITIES

Life is too short, and the Christian life too exciting, for us to waste our time on trivialities. T. S. Eliot, in one of his poems, describes a group of sophisticated people who measure out their lives "with coffee spoons." What a foolish way to live! Yet some Christians live that way.

One day each of us will have to give an account of his life to God. Jesus, when he gave his account, said: "I glorified Thee on the earth, having accomplished the work which Thou hast given Me to do" (John 17:4). I trust that I will be able to give that kind of report, and that you will, too.

One of the first steps toward making our lives "accountable" is to major on the priorities, the things that matter most. If we are going to overcome the world, we must abandon the world's standards for success. We must measure our lives by the things that God holds dear. We must ruthlessly cut away all that is excessive and that holds us back from doing God's will. "Let us also lay aside every encumbrance, and the sin which so easily entangles us, and let us run with endurance the race that is set before us" (Heb. 12:1).

We may not like to admit it, but too many believers (and Christian ministries) live by the code of the world. Instead of overcoming the world, they have been overcome by the world. Some of them have imitated the world in hope that they can attract the world, but their very success is failure. They have forgotten the priorities that make the Christian life distinctively Christian. Jesus reminds us of these priorities in this prayer that we have been studying.

1. *God's glory*

The prayer opens with a concern for God's glory: "Glorify Thy Son, that the Son may glorify Thee." Near the close of the prayer (v. 24), Jesus mentions this glory again. The very boundaries of the prayer are statements concerning the glory of God. As we have noted, the word "glory" is used in one way or another eight times in this prayer. This should not surprise us, because our Lord's greatest concern was that the Father be glorified.

Our Lord's incarnation helped to make visible some of the glory of God. "And the Word became flesh, and dwelt among us, and we beheld His glory, glory as of the only begotten from the Father, full of grace and truth" (John 1:14). His miracles "manifested His glory" (John 2:11). "I do not receive glory from men," he told the crowds (John 5:41). He was interested only in "the glory that is from the one and only God" (John 5:44). "If I glorify Myself, My glory is nothing; it is My Father who glorifies Me. . . ." (John 8:54).

Even the suffering of the cross was looked upon in terms of the glory of God. "The hour has come for the Son of Man to be glorified. . . . Father, glorify Thy name. . . ." (John 12:23, 28). When Judas deserted the upper room to consummate his business deal with the Sanhedrin, Jesus said, "Now is the Son of Man glorified, and God is glorified in Him; if God is glorified in Him; God will also glorify Him in Himself, and will glorify Him immediately"

(John 13:31–32). Imagine speaking about the glory of God at the very time a false friend was betraying him!

The lesson is obvious: everything that God permits in the life of the believer can be used to his glory. If we live to please ourselves, we will be constantly bored and disappointed; if we live to glorify God, we will overcome the world. The world cries, "Save yourself! That is the only way to happiness!" But Jesus says, "He who loves his life loses it; and he who hates his life in this world shall keep it to life eternal" (John 12:25). It is a costly thing to live for the glory of God, but it is even costlier not to. The words of martyred Jim Elliot come to mind: "He is no fool who gives what he cannot keep, to gain what he cannot lose."

"Whether, then, you eat or drink or whatever you do, do all to the glory of God" (1 Cor. 10:31).

2. *Truth*

We live in a deceived world because "the whole world lies in the power of the evil one" (1 John 5:19). People think they can see, but they are really blind. They have substituted prices for values, quantity for quality, and toys for tools. The cult of the immediate has conquered: immediate pleasure, immediate wealth, immediate success. Few people stop to ask, "Is what we are doing based on truth? Is it authentic? Is it real?"

The believer knows the "only true God" (John 17:3), and in knowing God he is better able to know himself and the world around him. The believer is in touch with reality, and this experience has radically altered his sense of values. Paul had this experience and recorded the results in Philippians 3: "But whatever things were gain to me, those things I have counted as loss for the sake of Christ. More than that, I count all things to be loss in view of the surpassing value of knowing Christ Jesus my Lord, for whom I have suffered the loss of all things, and count them but rubbish in order that I may gain Christ" (Phil. 3:7–8).

Jesus Christ is "the truth" (John 14:6), and we must love him. We must cultivate a personal relationship with Christ in worship, prayer, mediation, and obedience. This is the kind of communion he desires. "No longer do I call you slaves; for the slave does not know what his master is doing; but I have called you friends, for all things that I have heard from My Father I have made known to you" (John 15:15). The Word of God is truth (John 17:17), and as never before the believer needs to be saturated with the Word. "But his delight is in the law of the LORD, and in His law he meditates day and night" (Ps. 1:2). The Word enables us to see the world as it really is, and to avoid the snares which the adversary has set for us. We examine ourselves in the light of the Word and discover those areas that need spiritual therapy. "Sanctify them in the truth," prayed Jesus. "Thy word is truth" (John 17:17).

The Holy Spirit is the truth (1 John 5:7), and we must maintain a strong relationship with him. The Spirit speaks to us through the Word and through that inner judge, the conscience. Sometimes the Spirit speaks to us through other believers. The Bible commands us to "walk by the Spirit" (Gal. 5:16), to be "led by the Spirit" (Gal. 5:18), to produce "the fruit of the Spirit" (Gal. 5:22), and, in order to accomplish all of this, to be "filled with the Spirit" (Eph. 5:18).

We must be careful always to speak the truth in love (Eph. 4:15). Whenever a lie comes on the scene, there will be division and destruction. Satan is a master liar, and his lies place people in bondage. It is God's truth that sets us free (John 8:31–32). The world hates truth, and so the world hates Christians. "If they persecuted Me," said Jesus, "they will also persecute you; if they kept My word, they will keep yours also" (John 15:20). Note that it is the Word that makes the difference.

One of my pastor friends had as the motto for his church: "Always the Word." You can't improve on that! "Always the

Word"—in every Sunday school class, in the pulpit, in the choir selections, in the managing of the church business meetings and committee meetings, in the missionary outreach of the church, in the youth ministry, in the homes . . . *always the Word.* How tragic it is to see the saints being fed pabulum diets of religious entertainment when their souls cry out for the nourishment of the Word!

3. *Assurance*

If there is one message that comes across in this prayer, it is that God's people are secure in their relationship to Jesus Christ. Assurance is not something that we work *for*; it is something that we work *from.* How could we ever overcome the world if we were unsure of our relationship to God? Jesus Christ has already overcome the world (John 16:33), so we are fighting *from* victory, not *for* victory.

The doctrine of assurance is not an excuse for sin; it is an encouragement not to sin. The fact that I know I am married and have documents to prove it does not in the least tempt me to investigate other relationships. My wife and I are secure in our love for each other. When I realize the expensive grace that God has poured out on me, I want to draw closer to him and share his love even more. The fact that some professed Christians "turn the grace of God into licentiousness" (Jude 4), or decide to "continue in sin that grace might increase" (Rom. 6:1), should not rob us of the precious doctrine of assurance.

Knowing that we have been given to the Son by the Father ought to motivate us to loving obedience. We are the Father's love gift to Jesus! Knowing that he prayed for us when he was on earth, and that he now prays for us in glory, ought to encourage us to fight sin and be faithful to God. Knowing that his work is finished, that salvation is complete, ought to strengthen us in our warfare. Everything that God is, and everything that Christ has done and is now doing combines to produce in our hearts the kind of assurance that leads to holy living.

It is not enough to win people to Christ. We must also lead them into assurance, for only as they have assurance can they effectively live for God and overcome the world. Paul prayed that his friends in Colosse might attain "to all the wealth that comes from the full assurance of understanding" (Col. 2:2). The apostle John wrote, "These things I have written to you who believe in the name of the Son of God, in order that you may know that you have eternal life" (1 John 5:13).

4. *Obedience*

To begin with, Christ was obedient to the Father's will and accomplished his assigned work on the earth. In spite of their failures, the disciples received Christ's Word, kept it, and shared it with a lost world. We are enriched by the gospel today because other generations of believers were obedient to God's will.

The founder of the China Inland Mission, J. Hudson Taylor, once witnessed to a Chinese seeker. "How long have your people had this message?" the man asked, and Taylor told him, "Hundreds of years." "Then why did you not come sooner?" the seeker cried. "My father sought the truth his whole life and died without finding it!"

We have the truth, not to embalm it and "preserve" it, but to share it with a lost world. We have assurance, not so that we can become a religious elite, but so that we can witness to others who have no assurance. Truth and assurance are not ends in themselves; they are the means to the end of taking the gospel to the whole world. "As Thou didst send Me into the world," said Jesus, "I also have sent them into the world" (John 17:18).

Jesus finished the work the Father gave him to do, but his church has not yet finished the work that the Savior gave us to do. Our priorities are confused. We waste our financial and human resources on grandiose schemes that have little or no relationship to the commission God has given us. We are rearranging the furniture while the house is burning down. We are entertaining the saints when we ought to be evangelizing the sinners. To paraphrase Mark Twain, lies are running around while truth is still putting on her shoes.

True, we have sacrificed to build impressive buildings and outfit them, but "to obey is better than sacrifice" (1 Sam. 15:22). This does not mean that it is not God's will for us to erect sanctuaries and offices, but it is a reminder that such programs, even in the will of God, are not a substitute for obedience. God wants our sons and daughters—and ourselves—as much as he wants our silver and gold, and perhaps more, for if He has us, he will have everything.

5. *Unity*

"That they may be one" is a repeated burden in this prayer (vv. 21–23). The unity of God's people is an essential part of evangelism: "that the world may believe that Thou didst send Me" (v. 21). The unbiblical divisions and disputes among God's people hinder the progress of the gospel far more than we realize. The essence of the gospel is "God so loved," and it is difficult to share a loving gospel when the saints lack love for one another. The gospel speaks of the grace of God, but if the world does not see grace between Christians, how can they believe in the grace of God?

The unity that our Lord prayed for is not institutional or organizational. It is spiritual: "that they may be one, just as We are one" (v. 22). Unity grows from within; uniformity is forced from without. Unity is living; it grows and expands. Uniformity is dead and brittle, and the least jarring thing breaks it. Unity allows for variety and diversity, but uniformity demands conformity. Unity is based on love and thrives on love, but uniformity is defensive and is based too often on fear.

Again, it is a matter of priorities. Can we not allow for diversity in the body of Christ? Must we all have the same

149

form of church government, when history proves that God has blessed each form in one way or another? Must we all express our worship in the same forms? Must we all use the same methods for doing the work of God? Are not some things in the church more important than others?

"Away with all discriminating names," wrote the Puritan preacher Thomas Brooks. "Discord and division become no Christian. For wolves to worry the lambs is no wonder, but for one lamb to worry another, this is unnatural and monstrous."

Spiritual unity does not come naturally to God's people. We have to work at it. But are we working hard enough? Paul urged us to be diligent "to preserve [not manufacture] the unity of the Spirit in the bond of peace" (Eph. 4:3). Must we always have our way? Is our personal interpretation and application of the Bible always the right one? Is it possible that we are using the gospel ministry as a cover-up for giving vent to our own fears and frustrations? "Some, to be sure, are preaching Christ even from envy and strife . . . out of selfish ambition, rather than from pure motives. . . ." (Phil. 1:15, 17). We may not agree with such ministry, but, with Paul, let's rejoice that Christ is being preached.

There can be unity only when love and truth are joined together. Ministry that is motivated by love will encourage unity; ministry that is motivated by personal selfish gain will only create division. Human nature loves to exalt man: "'I am of Paul,' and 'I of Apollos,' and 'I of Cephas,' and 'I of Christ'" (1 Cor. 1:12). A lady said to me, "I am one of your fans!" I calmly replied, "I don't have a fan club." If she had said, "Your ministry has blessed my life" or "You have made me love the Word more," I would have rejoiced. After all, the minister's task is to get people to follow Christ, not the minister.

It will take a great deal of courage for us to start promoting spiritual unity. For one thing, we will be branded as "ecumaniacs," even though we are not endorsing the liberal ecumenical movement. Or we may be called "compromisers" because we dare to see some good in believers who disagree with us. So be it. Our Lord prayed for unity; this was a great priority in his life and ministry. It ought to be a priority to us.

Before leaving this theme, I must point out again that this spiritual unity is *something the world can see.* "And all those who had believed were together . . . praising God, and having favor with all the people" (Acts 2:44, 47). "And the congregation of those who believed were of one heart and soul . . . And with great power the apostles were giving witness to the resurrection of the Lord Jesus. . . ." (Acts 4:32–33). The oneness of the body was evident to the outsiders, and this gave the Christians opportunity for effective witness.

True spiritual unity is never at the expense of truth. We need to be reminded again of Augustine's counsel:

In essentials, unity;
in non-essentials, liberty;
in all things, charity.

6. *Holy living*
"Sanctify them in the truth; Thy word is truth" (v. 17).

How strange it is that we have so much Bible study and so little holy living. Some churches seem to promote material success rather than personal sanctification of life. We count our converts, but too often our converts don't count when it comes to devotion to Christ. The Christian who does seek to live a holy life is often isolated as an eccentric, a bit of an embarrassment to the church. After all, he doesn't join all the religious causes, attend all the seminars, or get excited about the religious celebrities who vie for the spotlight. Christians today are not looking for holiness; they're looking for happiness and success—measured, of course, on the world's terms.

Holy living is ceasing to be a requirement for pastoral ministry, in spite of what Paul wrote in 1 Timothy 3 and Titus 1. Church officers need not prove themselves before they are selected, nor do they have to prove faithful after they are in office. When a church pulpit is vacant, the pulpit committee rarely calls a prayer meeting. Usually it is a dinner meeting during which another committee is appointed to investigate the "great preachers" of the day to see if they might be interested in a change. Popularity is more important than character. Does the man pay his bills? Does he manage his household according to the Bible? Does he have a consistent devotional life? These questions are rarely asked.

In spite of the epidemic of "deeper life" conferences and books on "victory," we are not producing many saints. The visiting preacher who dares to preach on sin and holiness is rarely invited back. The pastor who emphasizes godliness week after week often sees the congregation dwindle and notes that the atmosphere in the church grows chilly. A book on holiness would not likely hit the best-seller list. After all, our "role models" for the successful Christian life today are not saints, but entertainers, people who claim they turn the nightclub into a church, but who end up turning the church into a nightclub. Ask the average Christian if he has ever gotten acquainted with Samuel Rutherford, Robert Murray McCheyne, Brother Lawrence, or even A. W. Tozer, and he will give you a blank look and a shake of the head. There has arisen a generation that knows not practical holiness.

All of these priorities hang together. Holy living is based on the truth, and the truth gives us assurance. This leads to obedience and promotes unity among the saints, which results in a strong witness to the world. The final result is that the Lord is glorified.

So, we must begin with personal holiness of life.

Can *one* Christian make a difference? Yes! God does not call committee meetings. He calls individuals to overcome the world and glorify his name. When he wanted to save a lost world, he called Abraham and founded the Hebrew nation. When he wanted to deliver that nation from bondage, he called Moses. He called Joshua to lead the nation into their inheritance, and Samuel and David to rescue the people when their sins had led them back into slavery. He called Paul to take the gospel to the Gentiles. He called Elisabeth to bear John the Baptist, and Mary to give birth to the Savior. He called Lydia to open up her home for the church at Philippi, and Priscilla and Aquila to befriend Apollos and Paul.

What are your priorities?

Are you a part of the problem, or a part of the answer?

Warren W. Wiersbe is Distinguished Professor of Preaching at Grand Rapids Baptist Seminary and has pastored churches in Indiana, Kentucky, and Illinois (Chicago's historic Moody Church). He is the author of more than 100 books, including *God Isn't in a Hurry, The Bumps Are What You Climb On,* and *the Bible Exposition Commentary* (2 vols.).